Editors

Erica N. Russikoff, M.A.

Brent L. Fox, M. Ed.

Editor in Chief

Karen J. Goldfluss, M.S. Ed.

Creative Director

Sarah M. Fournier

Cover Artists

Diem Pascarella

Barb Lorseyedi

Marilyn Goldberg

Imaging

Amanda R. Harter

Publisher

Mary D. Smith, M.S. Ed.

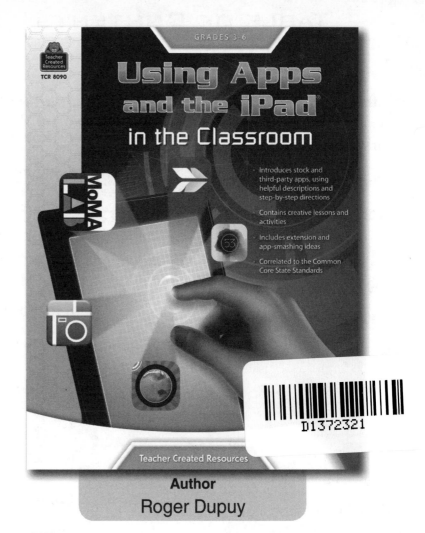

GRADES 3–6

TCR 8090

Using Apps and the iPad
in the Classroom

- Introduces stock and third-party apps, using helpful descriptions and step-by-step directions
- Contains creative lessons and activities
- Includes extension and app-smashing ideas
- Correlated to the Common Core State Standards

Teacher Created Resources

Author

Roger Dupuy

CORRELATED TO COMMON CORE STANDARDS

For correlations to the Common Core State Standards, see pages 93–94 of this book or visit *http://www.teachercreated.com/standards/*.

Teacher Created Resources

6421 Industry Way

Westminster, CA 92683

www.teachercreated.com

ISBN: 978-1-4206-8090-4

© 2015 Teacher Created Resources

Made in U.S.A.

Teacher Created Resources

TABLE OF CONTENTS

Using Apps and the iPad® in the Classroom is designed to help you create amazing, technology-enhanced lessons for your students. Whether you are a first-time or veteran user, this book suggests ways in which you can improve the overall classroom experience using an approachable, interactive tool.

The apps discussed in this book are divided into two categories: Stock Apps and Third-Party Apps. Stock apps are apps that Apple® provides for you. These apps come with each device or are Apple apps that can be downloaded for free from the App Store℠. They usually require Wi-Fi. Third-party apps are apps designed by other developers and can be downloaded from the App Store. These apps may require Wi-Fi and may cost a nominal fee. These recommended apps are well suited to help you deliver practical, engaging classroom lessons. In both the Stock Apps and Third-Party Apps sections, descriptions and sample lesson plans are provided.

Using Apps and the iPad® in the Classroom is your reference manual. The apps and lessons are tagged with handy descriptors to let you choose the right app for your specific curricular objectives. For example, all the app descriptions are tagged with a pedagogical context (e.g., whole class, individual, small group), grade level suggestions, and more.

In addition to extension activities, app-smashing suggestions are provided. These suggestions allow for multiple apps to be used in a single activity.

At the back of this book, you will find an index organized by these same tags. Apps are sorted by context, activity type, and alphabetically. Advice and tips for permissions, Wi-Fi, and iPad® care are also included.

Each lesson meets the digital content and collaboration components as well as other standards required by the Common Core State Standards. A list of these standards can be found on pages 93–94.

After familiarizing yourself with this book, you will find it to be an indispensable tool as you endeavor to grow in the area of technology-enhanced learning.

First Things First

Before introducing the iPad and apps in your classroom, you will want to make sure that you are properly prepared. This section contains a brief overview of basic iPad functions, including steps on how to take screenshots and suggestions for organizing and switching between apps. The importance of obtaining permissions from families and school sites is also discussed. Understanding the capabilities and the parameters of your iPad before introducing it as a tool in your classroom will only make your experience as a teacher easier.

To begin, check to see how strong the Wi-Fi signal is at your school. Most schools are not ready for hundreds of simultaneous Wi-Fi logins. If your iPad app is Wi-Fi-dependent, then your experience is directly affected by how strong your school's Wi-Fi signal is. If you are at a school with little or no Wi-Fi, then you need to use your iPad differently. Look for the Wi-Fi tag under each app description. Use apps that do not require Wi-Fi. If your school has a strong Wi-Fi connection, then you will be able to use all of the apps mentioned in this book.

WI-FI

Schools have varying policies when it comes to website accessibility. Get a current list from your network administrator. You will need to check this list to see if the websites you plan to use are approved by your school's network administrator.

In any case, be sure to test every website on your iPad, as certain websites with Adobe® Flash® Player may not function as expected, or possibly not at all.

WEBSITE PERMISSIONS

Find out the policy on students taking the iPad home with them. Your students may not be able to do this every day. If this is the case, what apps you use will be affected. The apps in this book are tagged with useful descriptors to help you filter through what you need based on available technology.

IPAD USE AND AVAILABILITY

Teacher Research

This is your basic research and preparation. This is not at all different from what you as a teacher normally do before and after class as part of your regular preparations. The only difference is that you are including your iPad as an additional tool.

TAGS BASED ON CONTEXT

Whole Class

This is your standard whole-class, teacher-led lesson context. You will need an LCD projector and a connection cable. You will only need one iPad for this.

Small Group

This is when you are leading a small group activity (usually 2–5 people). Each student should have his or her own iPad.

Individual

This is an individual student activity. The students are all working on their own individual mobile digital devices while the teacher monitors their progress. This could also be the context for a center activity.

Note: Certain iPad activities can be used in more than one context. Also, in many cases, the activities in this book progress from whole class, to small group, to independent classwork, and finally to homework, as this would likely reflect the natural flow of the lesson.

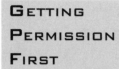

GETTING PERMISSION FIRST

Depending on your school district's policy, you may need to get written permission from parents to take pictures of their children to display in class. It is worth the effort, as there are very creative apps that use kids' pictures. Below is an example of a letter that you can send to parents to obtain written approval for camera use in the classroom:

Dear Parent or Guardian of _____,

Our class will be using various iPad apps during the school year. Some of the apps require the use of pictures and photos. With your permission, I would like to take photos of your child during classroom activities. These photos may be shown to other classes and administrators.

Please sign below, indicating whether or not you agree with _____ School using digital cameras and digital images of your child for the purpose of classroom instruction.

Thank you.

_____
Teacher Signature

☐ I approve of you taking photos of my child.

☐ I do not approve of you taking photos of my child.

Parent Signature

_____

Switching between apps, especially when you're working with multiple apps, is easy to accomplish.

Organizing apps will greatly help you in the classroom. Knowing where to look for a particular app will save you valuable instructional time.

By using the Spotlight® Search function, you can search for apps quickly and efficiently.

How to Switch Between Apps (Two Ways)

1. The first way to switch between apps is to double-tap the Home button. This calls up a switching interface. It shows you the apps in the order you last used them.

2. Swipe to the left to scroll to the app you want and then tap on it to launch it.

Or

The other way is to use a four-finger swipe from right to left while having an app open (not from the Home screen). This gesture takes you to the last app you were working on. This technique is best when you are trying to jump between two or three apps.

How to Organize Apps

1. From your Home screen, tap and hold an app until all the app icons wiggle.

2. Tap and drag an app into another to create a folder, which can then be named.

3. To move an app to another screen, drag the app or folder to the edge of the screen. Be sure not to tap on the X in the upper-left corner of the app icon. This will delete the app.

4. Once you are done moving and creating folders, push the Home button. The wiggling should stop.

Suggestion: Consider designating one entire screen for teacher preparation and research; one for live, in-class demonstrations; and one for personal/private use. Creating three spaces allows you to focus on the apps that directly help you in each context.

How to Use Spotlight Search to Search for Apps

1. From the Home screen, swipe down with one finger.

2. Type what app you need.

3. Select the app.

Note: You can also use Spotlight Search for Internet searches. Simply type in what you're looking for and tap on Search Web or Search Wikipedia™.

SCREEN CAPTURE

Use your iPad to take a screenshot of the current screen display. The image is automatically saved to your Camera Roll®.

How to Use Screen Capture to Take Screenshots

1. Decide on the display of which you wish to take a photo.

2. Push the Home button and the Power button at the same time. You should hear an audible camera-clicking sound.

3. The screenshot is automatically saved to your Camera Roll.

Suggestion: Consider using Screen Capture to showcase or evaluate student work. Have students take screenshots of their progress and email them to you.

SELECT, COPY, AND PASTE

Use your iPad to select, copy, and paste text.

How to Select, Copy, and Paste Text

1. One way you can select, copy, and paste text is to tap the text you want to copy, holding your finger down until you see a magnification bubble.

2. Slide the cursor until you've highlighted all the text you intend to copy, then lift your finger.

3. Select Copy.

4. Press and hold your finger at the location where you would like to paste the text.

5. Select Paste.

PROJECTING
IMAGES

IPAD
TROUBLESHOOTING

LET'S GET
TO THE APPS

The iPad can be used as a document camera. To do this, you will need a projector and either a VGA cable and Apple's VGA adapter or an HDMI cable and Apple's HDMI adapter.

If you don't want to hassle with connection cables, you can use Apple TV®. Apple TV is a small receiver that connects to your projector or TV via an HDMI cable. Using Wi-Fi, it wirelessly connects to your iPad using a feature called AirPlay®. For information on how to connect your iPad to an Apple TV, go to *http://support.apple.com/en-us/HT201335*.

Your iPad is very reliable; however, there are two common problems that your iPad may have. The first one can be referred to as the "Sudden Quit." This occurs when you are working in one of your apps and, suddenly, the app quits. If this happens, you will need to restart the app. During a "Sudden Quit," you may lose some of the data. (e.g., Some of your Pages® document might not have been saved.)

The second problem can be referred to as the "Freeze." This is when an app stops working, and no amount of tapping can unfreeze it. If this happens, try pushing the Home button first. If this doesn't work, push the Power button (at the top-right corner of your iPad). If neither of these work, then you will need to restart your device.

How to Restart Your Device

1. Hold the Power button until "slide to power off" appears. Follow these instructions. Once the device is off, press the Power button to turn it back on.

2. If you can't restart your device, reset it by pressing and holding the Power and Home buttons at the same time until the Apple logo appears.

Note: When all else fails, go to *support.apple.com* for the latest information on solving your issue.

Suffice it to say, the iPad has the foundational functionality to be a very useful tool. The rest of this book is designed to show how it can benefit you while suggesting apps, lessons, and activities that you can use in your classroom.

STOCK APPS

This section introduces features of stock apps for the iPad. Stock apps are apps that Apple provides for you. These apps come with each device or are Apple apps that can be downloaded for free from the App Store. They may require Wi-Fi. Learning how to use these stock apps will prepare you to most effectively implement the other apps introduced in this book.

MAIL

Description

Mail® is Apple's email program. The Mail app is essential to the functionality of the iPad because it is the main sharing mechanism. Upon receiving your iPad, set up one or more email accounts for classroom use.

How to Set Up a Mail (Email) Account

1. Launch the Settings app.

2. On the left side of the screen, select Mail, Contacts, Calendars.

3. Under the Accounts heading, select Add Account. Several email options will appear. The steps are slightly different depending on the account you wish to use. The next page explains how to set up a Gmail™ account.

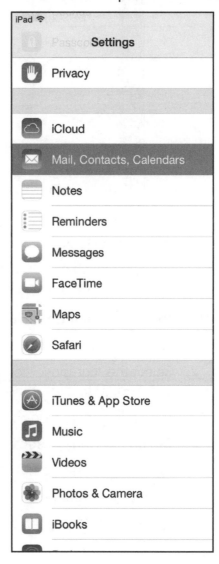

MAIL

How to Set Up a Mail (Email) Account *(cont.)*

   a. Select Google™ for a Gmail account.

   b. Enter your name, full email address, email password, and a short description.

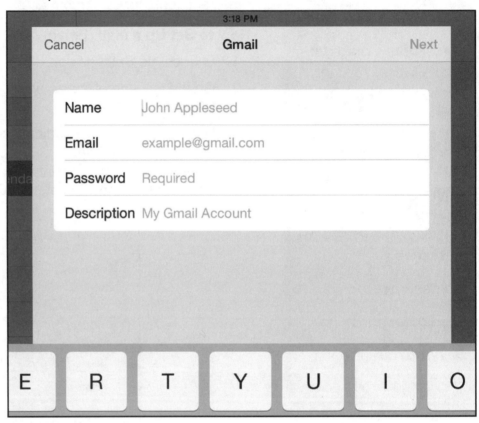

   c. Select Next.

   d. Decide which services you would like tied to your Gmail account. Toggle the button sliders once you've made your choices.

How to Send a Mail Email

1. Launch the Mail app.

2. Select the "compose" icon (it looks like a box with a pen pointing to the middle of it) to open a new Mail composing window.

3. Tap on the To section. Enter the email address of the recipient.

4. Tap on the Subject section. Enter your subject.

5. Type a short message. Remind your students to always include their names.

6. Review your email.

7. Tap the Send button in the upper-right corner of the composition window.

MAIL

Some Mail Tips

From within the Mail composing window, if you tap on From, you will be able to choose from all the email accounts (personal, work, etc.) you have set up on your iPad.

From the main Mail view screen, if you tap and hold (also known as a "long press") the Compose icon, all of your unsent drafts will appear.

Wi-Fi and Email

You can compose emails without a Wi-Fi connection. Once you are in a Wi-Fi hotspot, your emails will be sent automatically.

The Subject Line

Stress the importance of a strong subject line with your students. You will be getting plenty of emails, and you need to quickly determine from the subject line what the emails are about. Many of the apps in this book will require that your students send you attachments. It's important that they include subject lines to alert you to specific assignments.

Your Choice: One or Many Email Accounts

Decide whether you are going to have each of your students set up a separate email account or if you will only have a single email account for the whole class. Separate email accounts make more sense for older students. You still may need to set up each of their email accounts for them. This will likely take some time, but it's essential. Your students may not be too familiar with the iPad, and knowing how to send emails is one of the first things you need to teach them. Remember that many of the apps in this book require email to share and submit files. If you decide to use a single email account for the whole class, then you will still need to set up this email account on each iPad.

MAIL

Email Etiquette

Lesson Objective

Students will learn basic email etiquette and the difference between a friendly email and a business email. Students will be able to demonstrate email etiquette when presented with several different email scenarios.

Materials and Preparation

- one iPad per student
- one teacher iPad and projection or streaming technology
- Email Etiquette worksheet

Before teaching this lesson, teachers should create an Email Etiquette worksheet by compiling a list of five or six email scenarios for students to respond to. Each teacher should create scenarios that best meet the needs of his or her students, but here are some suggestions to get you started:

- an email from a friend asking to borrow a video game
- an email from a teacher asking for extra help before school
- an email from a grandparent sending birthday wishes
- an email from a local business looking for some help passing out flyers

Allow room under each scenario for students to provide examples of appropriate email responses using proper email etiquette.

Opening/Input

1. Share the lesson objective with the students.
2. Explain to students that email is a necessary form of communication, and using proper email etiquette is very important. In the same way that students are expected to behave differently in different scenarios, students should also treat emails in a similar way. Notes to adults, businesses, or regarding any matter of importance should be polite and proper. Notes to friends or siblings can be more casual and informal.
3. Discuss some important email etiquette tips. The list below includes just a few suggestions on topics you may want to discuss.
   - Use a proper greeting. Address the recipient with respect.
   - Spell the recipient's name correctly, and address him or her with Mr., Mrs., or Ms. when appropriate.
   - Keep the content of your email brief and to the point.
   - Be polite, and remember to always use "please" and "thank you."
   - Use correct spelling, grammar, and punctuation. Unless you are writing an informal email, avoid using slang terms and emoticons. Smiley faces and LOLs don't belong in a formal email.
   - Before sending, make sure you have addressed your email correctly and your subject line clearly states what the email is about.
   - Avoid using "Reply All" and "Forward" unless absolutely necessary.

MAIL

Guided Practice

1. Project an email for the entire class to see. The email can be something simple, such as a brief letter from the library inquiring about the whereabouts of an overdue book. Ask a volunteer to read the email aloud to the rest of the class.

2. Discuss what type of email this is and how it should be properly addressed. Formally? Informally? What is the person in the email requesting?

3. Brainstorm ideas on how to properly respond to the email. On a graphic organizer, list all the important ideas shared by the class. Students should be providing information about the layout, content, spelling, and tone of the email.

4. With the help of the class, construct a response to the original email. Discuss each relevant etiquette tip as you apply it to the letter.

On Their Own

1. Distribute your Email Etiquette worksheet to each student.

2. Have students complete the worksheet independently. Remind students that this is a writing activity and that they should be applying as many good etiquette tips as possible. Informal emails to friends should have a much different look and tone than other emails.

3. When students have finished their worksheets, have them switch papers and read at least two responses from other students. Allow students time to make any changes to their own worksheets before turning them in.

Extensions and App-Smashing

- Invite teachers or parents to send emails to the class, and allow students to practice responding to their notes. Similarly, students can write notes to teachers, parents, or even local businesses, and then discuss and critique the responses when they arrive.

- Produce several examples of emails that do not model proper email etiquette. Ask students to correct and rewrite the emails.

- Using a photo-labeling app such as Skitch, allow students to take a poorly written email and label all the parts that need to be addressed. Save each image to a shared classroom file so students can use it for reference in the future.

MAIL

Sending and Receiving Attachments

This is one of the primary ways to get data in and out of the iPad. The files going in and out are called attachments. The following instructions explain how to send files that you want to share.

How to Send Image Files

1. Launch the Photos® app. In the upper-left corner, you can view your photos by Moments, Collections, and Years.

2. Select a photo from Moments.

3. Tap on the "share" icon (it looks like a box with an arrow pointing out of the top of it). A tray of icons representing all your sharing options will appear.

4. Select the "Mail" icon and proceed with sending your email.

How to Send Notes

1. Launch the Notes® app. Create a document.

2. Select the "share" icon in the upper-right corner of the screen.

3. Select the "Mail" icon and proceed with sending your email.

How to Send Files from Pages, Keynote®, and Numbers®

1. Launch the Pages (Apple's word-processing app), Keynote (Apple's presentation app), or Numbers (Apple's spreadsheet app) app. Create a document.

2. Select the "share" icon in the upper-right corner. Choose Send a Copy. A tray of icons representing your sharing options will appear.

3. Select the desired format. Pages will give you format choices such as Pages, PDF, Word®, or ePub. Keynote will give you format choices such as Keynote, PDF, or PowerPoint®. Numbers will give you format choices such as Numbers, PDF, Excel®, or CSV.

4. Select the "Mail" icon and proceed with sending your email.

How to Open Files Received Via Email

1. Launch the Mail app, and select an email that has an attachment.

2. Press and hold the "attachment" icon. A pop-up menu will display a list of apps capable of opening the attachment (i.e., Mail, Pages, Google Drive™).

3. Select the app you want to use to open the file.

Description

Your iPad has a stock Clock® app with a built-in timer. Use it to time the activities in your lessons. There is a quick way to get the timer to launch.

How to Launch the Clock App

1. On the iPad screen, swipe up to see the Settings tray.

2. Select the "clock" icon on the right side of the tray.
3. Within the big circle, swipe up or down to set the minutes and/or hours.
4. Press the Start button on the left.

Or

1. Select the Clock app.
2. Select Timer in the bottom-right part of the screen.
3. Continue with steps 3–4 above.

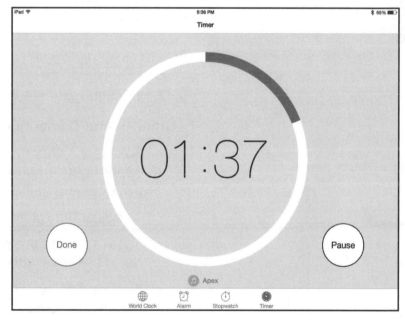

Note: You can choose different alarm tones by selecting the center "music note" icon.

CAMERA

Description

The Camera® app is one of the most important apps included on the iPad because of its universality. You can use the Camera app to take regular-sized or square pictures (including self portraits) and regular or time-lapse videos. The Camera app can also be used as a document camera.

How to Take Pictures and Videos

1. Power on your iPad, using either the Power button on the upper-right corner or the Home button on the bottom front of your iPad.

2. Swipe up the small "camera" icon located in the bottom-right corner of the screen.

3. Select whether you want to take a time-lapse video, regular video, regular photo, or square photo.

4. Compose your shot. For photos, zoom in using the slider bar at the bottom of the screen, or by placing two fingers onto the screen and spreading them apart.

5. Tap the large dot on the right of the screen (white for photo, red for video).

6. The photo or video is now saved to your Camera Roll. You can access this photo or video from the Photos app.

Or

1. Launch the Camera app.

2. Continue with steps 3–6 above.

Other Useful Camera Features

- To take a self-portrait, tap the "camera switch" icon in the upper-right corner of the screen. This will switch from the back camera to the front camera.

- To adjust the lighting, tap on the subject or area of focus.

- To take successive snapshots automatically, tap and hold down the large white dot while taking a picture.

- To take a delayed picture, tap on the "timer" icon on the right of the screen.

TAGS

Free

Classroom Contexts:
Whole Class, Teacher Research, Individual, Small Group

Wi-Fi: not required

Grades: all

Prerequisites: none

Developer: Apple Inc.

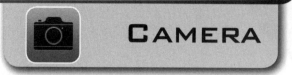

Video

The camera can shoot video footage as well. Just scroll to the "video" setting on the right side of the screen, just below the big circular button.

Time-Lapse and Slow Motion

The Camera app also offers a few other fun video-shooting modes: time-lapse and slow motion (slow motion is available on the iPad Air® and iPad mini™ with Retina® display). To use these modes, just swipe to the desired setting on the right side of the camera screen below the big circular button.

Practical Advice About Using Video

Here's a word of caution with videos. If you plan on sharing your videos, try to keep the videos under one minute in length. If your video needs to be longer, then break it up into a series of one-minute videos as you are shooting. This is important to remember for two reasons:

1. The first reason pertains to time management. You don't want to spend your time sending partial videos to recipients. It doubles your work and requires tremendous organization. It also takes more time for video production: creation, editing, and sharing. The longer the video is, the longer all these other processes take. Keep it under a minute—you'll be glad you did.

2. The second reason is pedagogical. What needs to be taught, assessed, or displayed can typically be accomplished in under a minute. Keeping videos under a specified time is a great exercise in getting to the point and communicating efficiently.

DICTIONARY

Description

Although not an app, this feature allows you to highlight any text on the iPad and look it up using Dictionary®.

How to Search for the Definition of a Word

1. Highlight a word by either double-tapping it or pressing and holding it.

2. Select Define from the pop-up options.

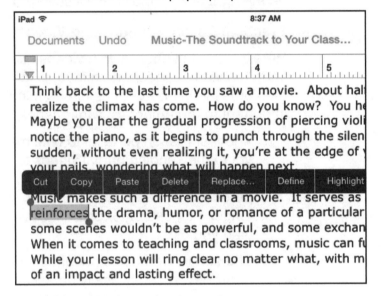

3. A pop-up window with a detailed dictionary definition will appear. Scroll down for more details on the entry, including etymology.

TAGS

Free

Classroom Contexts: Whole Class, Teacher Research, Individual, Small Group

Wi-Fi: optional (only needed to download extra dictionaries and languages)

Grades: all

Prerequisites: familiarity with Pages app

Developer: Apple Inc.

Double-Tap Dictionary Word Search

Lesson Objective

Students will learn how to use the stock dictionary feature to get definitions of teacher-selected vocabulary words.

Materials and Preparation

- one iPad per student
- one teacher iPad and projection or streaming technology

Using Pages, prepare a list of ten vocabulary words of which your students need to learn the definitions. Display the list from your iPad onto a screen using a projector.

Opening/Input

1. Share the lesson objective with the class, and discuss the importance of using a dictionary when reading and writing. Explain how technology has changed the look of the classic dictionary, but the function remains the same.

2. Open the Pages document that lists your ten vocabulary words. Use the projector to display the Pages word list.

3. For each vocabulary word, show how to double-tap a word to get the pop-up menu with the Define feature. Select Define.

4. Read the definition, and then tap on the Pages document next to the vocabulary word and record the definition from memory. You may have to double-tap on the vocabulary word more than once to verify the definition.

Guided Practice

Email students a Pages document containing ten difficult vocabulary words. Ask students to use the dictionary feature to define each word, and then include each word in a sentence. Ask several students to share their sentences.

On Their Own

1. Email a paragraph to students containing at least ten difficult (underlined) words.

2. Ask students to define each difficult word using Dictionary, and then rewrite the paragraph using the new definitions.

3. When they have finished, students can email the rewritten paragraphs to you.

Extension

Show your students how to use the stock dictionary feature in other cases. For instance, any website text can be highlighted and looked up using this feature. Press and hold the word to pop up the Define option.

SAFARI

Description

Safari® is Apple's Web browser. Use it to search the Web for information.

How to Use Safari

1. Launch the Safari app.

2. Tap on the URL window and type in a Web address or search term.

Safari Features

In the upper-left corner, you will find the backward and forward arrows, as well as the "Bookmarks" icon. The Bookmarks feature allows you to save websites to your Favorites or Reading Lists. It also stores any Shared Links, which are links shared by your contacts from specific social networks.

Safari Features *(cont.)*

Inside the URL window is the "reload" icon, followed by the "share" icon. If you tap on the "share" icon (it looks like an arrow pointing up inside a box), a tray of icons representing all your sharing options will appear. Tap on this icon to bookmark or add a site to your Reading List.

Select the "plus" icon to view an additional website. To view all of your websites at once, select the icon with overlapping squares.

Saving Images and Text

While you are browsing, you can tap on and hold almost any image to save it to the Camera Roll. You can also highlight and copy text to paste into other apps.

SAFARI

Creating Shortcut Icons

You can create a shortcut icon for any website you frequent. This is particularly useful when you are preparing a lesson and would like to have all of your websites in one place. You can create a folder on the Home screen with all the shortcut icons you need. Having a shortcut icon saves time. Instead of launching Safari and selecting a bookmark, you can just tap on the desired shortcut icon on your Home screen.

How to Create a Shortcut Icon

1. When you are viewing the website for which you want to have a shortcut, tap on the "share" icon.

2. Select the Add to Home button.

3. A pop-up window will appear, allowing you to edit the title of your new shortcut icon. Once you've decided on a title, select Add.

Protecting Your Students from Websites with a Lot of Clutter

Some websites are very cluttered with extraneous text, ads, and other distractions. You can instantly clean up the viewing interface by selecting the Reader button (it looks like a set of horizontal lines) that is inside and to the left of the URL text window.

Note: Not all websites work with this.

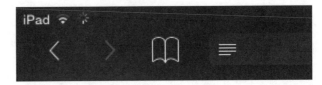

SAFARI

Gathering Information/Research

Lesson Objective

Students will create Pages documents, search the Internet for pictures, and then add the pictures to the Pages documents.

Materials and Preparation

- one iPad per student
- one teacher iPad and projection or streaming technology

Prepare a shortcut icon of the website *http://animalphotos.info* or any other photo-rich website containing animals.

Opening/Input

1. Tell students, "Today we're going to go on an animal safari. We're going to see animals from around the world, but we'll be able to do it without leaving our desks!" Discuss the Internet as a resource for information, including photographs.

2. Show students various photographs of animals by browsing through the animal website chosen in Materials and Preparation.

3. Choose an animal and save the image to your Photo Library. Share your thinking process as you walk the students through each step.

4. Create a Pages document.

5. Type the name of the animal at the top of the document using 16-point font.

6. Add the image of the animal to your document by tapping on the "plus" icon and selecting the "landscape" icon (it looks like a mountain and the sun inside of a rectangle). Select Recently Added. Then select the picture.

7. With the help of the students, write a paragraph below the photograph, describing the physical features of the animal and its environment.

8. Rename the document [your name]'s [animal] (ex. Mrs. Stempson's Red Panda).

9. Email the document to a friend or a classroom mailbox (previously created).

Guided Practice

Have a student volunteer go through this entire process again with his/her animal of choice. Use the four-finger app switching technique to quickly switch from the Web to the document and back again.

On Their Own

1. Project your Pages document as an example, including the URL of the photography website.

2. Set the iPad timer for an appropriate amount of time for your students to find and save the images of two <u>different</u> animals to their Photo Libraries.

On Their Own *(cont.)*

3. Ask students to add one image to their Pages documents, include the name of the animal in 16-point font, and then write paragraph-long descriptions about the animal's physical features and its environment.

4. Tell students to scroll to a second page and repeat the same steps with their second animal image. Be sure they add a title and a descriptive paragraph.

5. On the third page of their Pages document, have students add both images to the top of the page. Below the side-by-side images, explain to students that they are to write a paragraph comparing and contrasting the two animals. Encourage them to focus on as many similarities and differences as they can.

6. Ask students to rename the document [your name]'s [animals] (ex. Suzy's Red Panda and Polar Bear).

7. Finally, when they have completed the activity, have students email you the document in order to receive credit for the assignment.

Extensions and App-Smashing

• Challenge your students by having them find three animals that are similar. Have them attach photos of all three animals and then write several paragraphs discussing their similarities.

• Send your students the URL via email first, and have them go to the URL from within the Mail app.

• Ask each student to email his or her report to at least two classmates. Classmates can proofread, comment, and send the document back to the original author.

PAGES

TAGS

Free

Classroom Contexts:
Whole Class, Teacher
Research, Individual,
Small Group

Wi-Fi: optional (for
sharing files)

Grades: all

Prerequisites:
familiarity with Mail app

Developer: Apple Inc.

App Version: 2.5.2

Description

Pages is Apple's word processor. Its simple interface makes it ideal for young writers. Learning how to use Pages is important, as it is the foundation for many of the other lessons and activities in this book.

How to Use Pages as a Word Processor

1. Launch the Pages app.

2. Select Create Document.

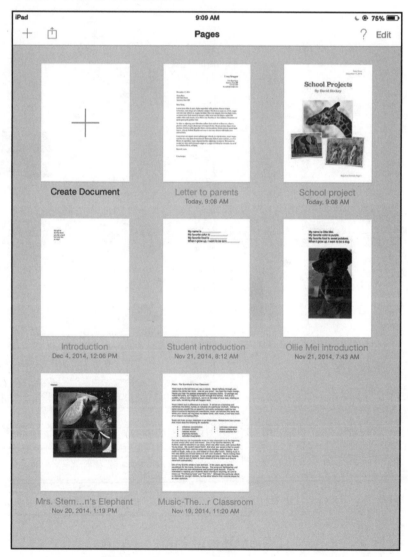

PAGES

How to Use Pages as a Word Processor *(cont.)*

3. Choose a template.

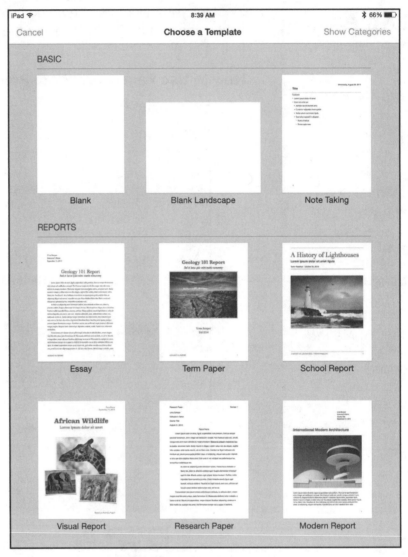

4. Rename the file by tapping on Blank and adding your own file name.

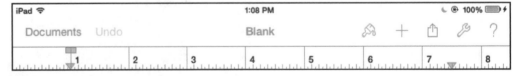

Other Useful Pages Features

- For simple formatting, select the options at the bottom of the screen. Alternatively, you can select the "paintbrush" icon in the upper-right corner of the screen.

- Pages automatically saves. To view or revise an existing document, you must first access the file system.

PAGES

How to Access the File System in Pages

1. Launch the Pages app or select Documents in the upper-left corner of the screen from within the Pages app. All of your documents will appear as thumbnails.

2. Tap on the file you want to open.

Note: To rename a file, tap on the file name.

How to Create Document Folders in Pages

1. Launch the Pages app or select Documents in the upper-left corner of the screen from within the Pages app. All of your documents will appear as thumbnails.

2. Tap and hold one of the documents and hover it over another document. A folder will appear.

3. Release your finger to drop the document into the folder.

4. Rename the folder by typing in the white text box.

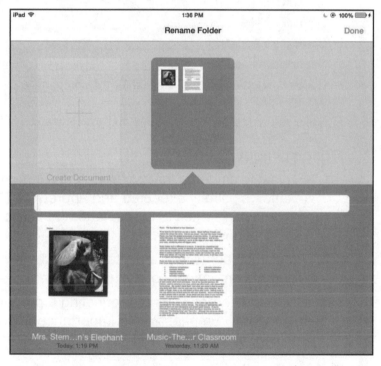

5. Tap outside the folder to close it.

How to Add an Image to a Pages Document

1. Select the "plus" icon in the upper-right corner of the screen.

2. Select one of the Albums.

3. Choose an image.

4. Drag and resize the image as needed.

PAGES

Writing a Formal Letter

Lesson Objective

Your students will use a Pages letter template to create a formal letter to a real company. Students will learn how to create a text document and learn how to do basic formatting using a premade template.

Materials and Preparation

- one iPad per student
- one teacher iPad and projection or streaming technology

Prepare a Classic Letter Worksheet (you can use the example below) using Pages.

Classic Letter Worksheet

Your Name: _____

Your Address: _____

Your Phone Number: _____

Your Email: _____ Date: _____

Company's Name: _____

Company's Address: _____

Name of Contact: _____ (You can just write: Dear Sir/Madam)

Content of Letter: Make a request for the company to send you a catalog of products that they sell.

Make sure you provide your name and your signature at the end of the letter.

Opening/Input

1. Explain to students that when writing a letter to a company, a certain style of letter is usually expected and appreciated by the recipient. Today they will be using Pages to create letters to fictitious companies and then to real local businesses.

2. Provide students with a digital Classic Letter Worksheet and discuss the different components of a classic letter.

3. Discuss different ways of requesting a product or information from a company. Emphasize the importance of proper grammar, correct spelling, and concise writing.

Guided Practice

1. Guide students through the digital worksheet, and answer any questions they may have. For the purpose of this lesson, fictitious information is acceptable.

2. After completing the worksheet, return to the first screen in Pages, and open a new Classic Letter template. Students can now cut the information from their Classic Letter Worksheets and paste it into the provided template.

Guided Practice *(cont.)*

3. Have a student volunteer demonstrate the process from the beginning a second time if there is a need.

On Their Own

1. Ask students to think of companies that they would like to learn more about or that they would like to receive catalogs from.

2. Have each student launch the Pages app and use the Classic Letter template to create his or her own letter to a real business.

3. Students may need to use Safari to find the correct addresses of the companies to which they are writing.

4. After giving the students an opportunity to proofread and edit their letters, print them and help students mail them to the companies.

Extensions

- Allow students to create envelopes from one of the options in the template array. They can use these envelopes for their business letters.

- If a student receives a response or a requested product from a company, have him or her write a thank-you letter using proper formatting and letter etiquette.

- Have students create brochures of real or imaginary places using the Brochure template in the Pages template array. Students should fill in the information about the places using either real or imaginary data.

Creating an Open-House Invitation

Lesson Objective

Students will create their own unique invitation posters inviting their parent(s)/guardian(s) to an Open House event. Students will learn how to create real invitations using images and the Pages template feature.

Materials and Preparation

- one iPad per student
- one teacher iPad and projection or streaming technology

Before teaching the lesson, the teacher should be familiar with the details of the school's Open House (date, time, etc.).

Opening/Input

1. Discuss with students the importance of clear communication. When sending an invitation, it is very important to pay close attention to the details.
2. Discuss what details should be included in an Open House invitation. What information should NOT go in the invitation?
3. Explain how they will be using Pages to create unique invitation posters. If students have never used Pages before, demonstrate the skills they will need to complete the assignment.

Guided Practice

1. Ask students to launch the Pages app.
2. Show students how to create an invitation using the School Poster Small template from the provided options. Ask students to show you how to add photos or insert text.
3. To check for understanding, have students demonstrate to partners how to add and delete photos, add text, and edit text.

On Their Own

1. Each student will create his or her own Open House invitation using one of the posters from the template array.
2. Print the students' invitations, and then send the invitations home to share with their parents.

Extensions and App-Smashing

- Have students email their invitations to one another to proofread. Students should respond with corrections, positive feedback, and at least one suggestion for improvement.
- Students can email their invitations to their family and friends. Encourage the families to RSVP with email responses.

iMOVIE

Description

iMovie® is Apple's video-editing and movie-making app. Teachers will likely find this app to be an enjoyable, yet effective teaching tool. While this app is user friendly and intuitive in its design, it may still be a bit challenging for some students. Additional assistance may be necessary.

Any photo or movie shared to the Photo Library or taken by your iPad can be used in iMovie. Also, iMovie has preloaded stock music, sound effects, and visual effects available for use in your movie creation. You can also download other music via your iTunes® account.

The app's interface reveals just enough detail for the basic functionality. If you want to utilize other, more advanced features, they can be easily accessed and are not too difficult to navigate. The information and steps provided here are designed to introduce the basic features of the app in small, manageable pieces.

There are two basic ways to use iMovie—as an iMovie Project and as a Trailer.

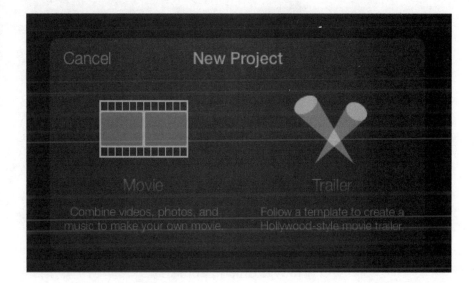

iMOVIE

How to Create a Movie

1. Launch the iMovie app.

2. Tap on the "plus" icon in the upper-right corner of the screen.

3. Select Movie.

4. Select one of the templates displayed at the bottom of the screen. iMovie gives you an array of templates to choose from. To see a preview of each, highlight the desired template and tap the "play" icon. Beginners may want to start with the Simple template.

5. In the upper-right corner of the screen, select Create. This is the basic movie editing screen.

6. Tap on Photos to search through the images in your Photo Library. After finding a photo to include in your movie, tap on the image to move it to your project timeline at the bottom of the screen.

7. Similarly, tap on Video to choose from prerecorded movie clips. Tap the "play" icon to preview the video, or tap the downward arrow to add it to your timeline.

IMOVIE

How to Create a Movie *(cont.)*

8. Locate where the "undo" icon is. It looks like a U-turn arrow. It is located on the right side of the screen, just above the project timeline. Use it whenever you want to undo the last thing you did.

9. At any point you want to remove a photo or video clip, you can also use the Delete feature. First, tap on the photo or video in the bottom timeline that you would like to remove. When the item is highlighted, tap on the "scissors" icon in the bottom-left corner of the screen. Three options will appear in the bottom-right of the screen: Split, Duplicate, and Delete. Tap on Delete to make the selected item disappear.

10. You can change the order of your video clips and photos by holding down your finger on the image and dragging it to a different place on the timeline. (You can do this with audio clips as well).

11. Preview your movie by pressing the "play" icon at the beginning of the timeline.

Note: Your movie is still in the project mode. This means that your movie can still be edited. You can share this current version at any time; however, once this current version is shared, the shared version cannot be edited anymore. Remember that you still have your original "project" available to edit and share as a different, perhaps more complete, version later.

iMOVIE

Sharing Your iMovie

Tap on the "arrow" icon in the upper-left part of the screen. Next, tap on the My Movie text to rename your movie project. From here you can choose from several icons: "play," "share," "delete," or you can return to the "editing" mode.

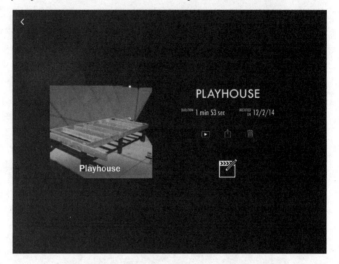

To share this project, select the "share" icon (it looks like an arrow pointing up inside a box). You will have the option to share your movie project to iMovie Theater®, Facebook, YouTube™, Vimeo, Messages®, or Mail, as well as your own Photo Library or iTunes account.

Various Sharing Options

Sharing to YouTube

This works great with finished movie projects that are too large to send via email. In order to save to YouTube, you will need to first set up a free YouTube video channel account. Once this is done, you can send URLs to others wanting to view your videos. If you prefer to keep your videos private, you can make them accessible only to the recipient of the URL generated by YouTube.

iMOVIE

Various Sharing Options *(cont.)*

Sharing to Vimeo

Similar to YouTube, Vimeo allows the user to post private videos and send customized URLs to others. Vimeo caters to a generally higher quality set of hosted videos.

Sharing to Facebook

Users must have a Facebook account before posting or sharing videos on this site. Facebook is not recommended for school policy reasons (school blacklists, etc.), and it's very hard to make the hosted videos private. Sharing to Facebook is not recommended for these reasons.

Sharing to iMovie Theater

This is a great option if you have a school iCloud® account. The videos shared to iMovie Theater are available to anyone who shares the same iCloud account. Using iMovie Theater with your personal iCloud account is not recommended. You will soon run out of hosting space.

Sharing to iTunes

Sharing to iTunes has the same issues as iMovie Theater. You don't want to get in the habit of using your personal accounts for potentially large iMovie files.

Sharing as a Message

For school purposes, this option is not advised.

Going Deeper

You can edit your project by adding more photos and video clips, changing the length of these clips, and adding audio files and sound effects. You can also add text to your movie, adjust transitions, slow down or speed up a clip, zoom in and crop your video clips and photos, and more. Let's explore some of these fun features.

Trimming Video Clips

If you want to trim the length of a video clip to edit out extraneous footage, first highlight the clip by tapping on the image in the timeline at the bottom of the screen. You should see a yellow box around the image. Next, place your finger on the left, heavy, yellow-colored bar and drag it to the right to exclude footage at the beginning of the clip; drag your finger on the right, heavy, yellow-colored bar to the left to exclude footage at the end of the clip. If you need to trim out footage in the middle of a clip, use the white line as a guide and drag the clip close to where you want to trim out footage. Make sure the clip is highlighted, and then select the Split button at the bottom of the screen. This splits the original clip into two clips. Then, just as above, use the yellow bars on the right and left of the clip to cut out undesired footage.

iMOVIE

Adding Text to Your Movie

Tap on a movie clip or photo in your timeline. Next, tap on the "text" (T) icon in the bottom-left corner of the screen. Several formatting options will appear on the bottom of the screen. Choose the format you wish to use by tapping on the appropriate box. "Title Text Here" will appear over your image, prompting you to replace the words with your own personalized text. Tap the "play" icon to preview your added text.

Adding Audio to Your Movie

More than likely, your video clips already contain sound from the original recordings. If you want to keep the original audio, you don't need to do anything. However, if you'd like to add to or replace the existing audio, you can easily add a voice-over audio clip. Here's how it is done.

How to Add a Voice-Over Audio Clip

1. Swipe your finger to any location on your timeline. Tap the "microphone" icon in the bottom-right corner of the app, and a recording prompt will appear.

2. Tap Record, and a countdown to record your voice will begin. Start speaking after the word Recording appears.

3. When you are done, select Stop. This gives you four options: Accept, Review, Retake, and Cancel.

4. Select Accept to add your voice-over to your timeline.

5. Select Review to hear how your voice-over will sync with the rest of the timeline.

6. Select Retake to start the recording process over again. The previous voice-over will be deleted.

7. Select Cancel to remove the voice-over prompt and return to the iMovie editing screen.

How to Adjust the Volume Level of the Audio Clip

1. Tap on a clip in the timeline.

2. Select Audio in the bottom-left corner of the screen. You can raise or lower the audio volume of the clip. Just slide the volume level left or right to decrease or increase the volume.

How to Use the Fade Feature

The Fade feature gives you the ability to gradually increase or decrease the volume at the beginning or end of a clip. If your iMovie video clip finishes before the music, you will likely want to fade out the music (or else the sudden end of your movie can be a bit jarring). Just slide the downward-facing triangles to taper the volume.

Trimming Your Audio Clips

The audio clip can be trimmed in the same way as a video clip.

How to Detach the Audio from the Video Clip

1. Tap on a video clip in the timeline.

2. Select the "scissors" icon in the bottom-left corner of the screen, then tap Detach in the bottom-right corner of the screen. The audio and the video files are now two separate files. You can now adjust the volume and speed up or slow down the clip to create funny effects. (However, the main reason for detaching audio from a video clip is to pair the audio with a different video clip or photo on your timeline and have it act, in effect, as a voice-over.)

Adding Other Audio Types: Music and Sound Effects

Select Audio in the upper-right corner of the app. All of your sound and music options will appear below.

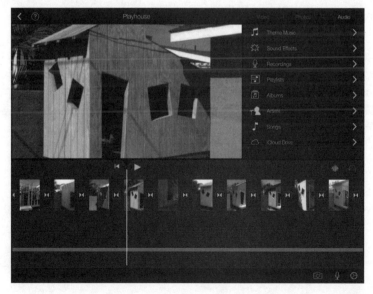

iMovie

How to Add Background Music from the Stock Templates

1. Tap on Theme Music and select a theme. You can preview it by tapping on the "play" icon.

2. If you like it, you can tap on the downward arrow icon. A green-colored audio clip image will now appear on your timeline. (You can now edit this audio clip in the same way you can edit other audio clips.)

Adding Sound Effects to Your Timeline

There are more than 60 stock sound effects included in iMovie. To add a sound effect, swipe your finger to move your timeline to the exact spot where you want to add a sound. Next, choose a sound effect and either press the "play" icon to preview it, or tap the downward arrow icon to add it to your timeline.

Adding Music to Your Timeline

You can also add sound recordings created with other apps, as well as imported or downloaded music (organized by playlist, album, artist, or song from your iTunes library).

iMovie Project Ideas for Teachers

Student and Classroom Portfolios

Any screenshot you take on your iPad can be added to your iMovie project timeline. Take screenshots of your students' completed work over time, and you can drop these photos into your timeline to create a student portfolio montage. Similarly, you can create a classroom portfolio montage by dropping in photographs of all the different assignments and projects completed throughout the year. Play the iMovie at year end to celebrate the students' progress.

Instructional Videos

Create a step-by-step instructional video of a long-term project by showing each step and recording a voice-over explaining the various stages of the project. Post the video online as a way for students and parents to preview a project, or as an instructional guide to be used while completing a project.

iMovie

How to Create a Trailer Using iMovie

1. Launch the iMovie app.

2. Tap on the "plus" icon in the upper-right corner of the screen.

3. Select Trailer.

4. Select one of the templates displayed at the bottom of the screen. iMovie gives you an array of movie themes to choose from (Superhero, Adrenaline, Family, etc.). To see a preview of each, highlight the desired template and tap the "play" icon. The length of the movie trailer and the suggested number of "actors" are displayed under the selected trailer.

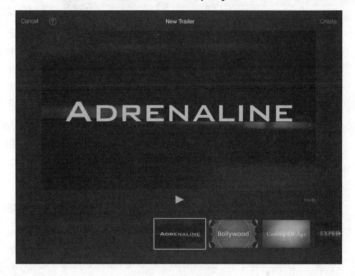

5. In the upper-right corner of the screen, select Create. This will take you to the trailer Outline and Storyboard.

6. Tap on each line in the Outline to customize the credits screen, including the name of the movie, the name of the studio, and the names of the people involved.

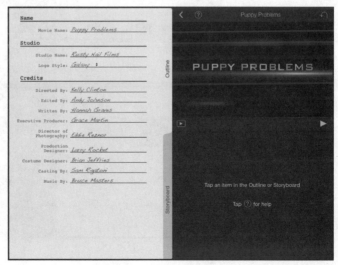

iMOVIE

How to Create a Trailer Using iMovie *(cont.)*

7. After you have completed your credits page, tap on the Storyboard tab. Here you will see a scene-by-scene breakdown of the entire trailer. To add text, tap on the blue highlighted lines and replace the existing text. You can use the original text as a guide to help you develop your own story.

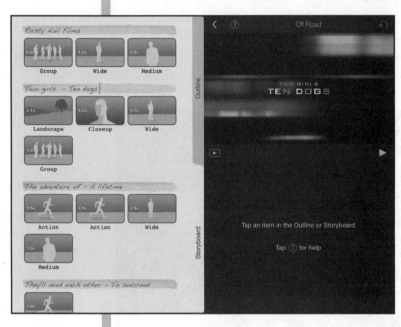

8. Next, tap on one of the gray photo boxes on the left to highlight it in blue. On the right half of your screen, you will be given several options from where you can choose what photos or videos you would like to use. In the bottom-right corner, you will see three choices: Video, Photos, and Camera. Tap on Video if you would like to add a video clip, or tap on Photos if you would prefer to add a still image.

9. To use an existing photo or video, tap on the image, and it will be added to the highlighted box.

If you would like to use a new video or photo, choose Camera and then proceed to use the Camera as you normally would. After you take a new video or photo, the scene will automatically be added to your trailer. To delete the video or photo, tap on the new image and then the "trash" icon.

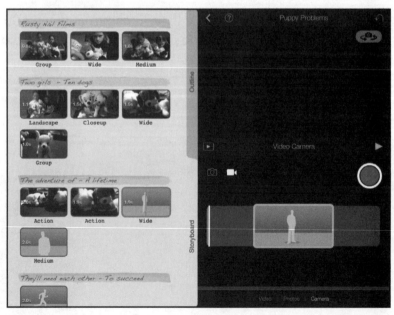

iMOVIE

How to Create a Trailer Using iMovie *(cont.)*

10. To edit a photo or video once it has been placed onto the storyboard, tap the image on the storyboard to bring up the editing screen on the right side of the page. Follow the directions on the screen to fine-tune photos and videos. Swipe with one finger to move the position of the photo, and pinch with two fingers to zoom in and out. For videos, swipe with one finger to adjust which portion of the clip is used.

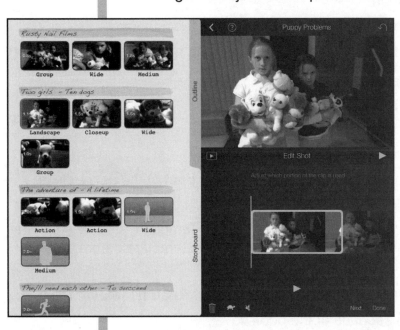

11. Add and delete text, photos, and videos until you have filled every space on the storyboard. You can tap the "play" icon at any point during the construction of your trailer to view its current status.

12. When you have finished, tap on the "arrow" icon in the top center of the screen. Your trailer is now complete (although it can still be edited). From here, you can choose from several icons: "play," "share," "delete," or you can return to the "editing" mode. To share this project, select the "share" icon. You will have the option of sharing your movie project to iMovie Theater, Facebook, YouTube, Vimeo, Messages, or Mail, as well as your own Photo Library or iTunes account.

iMovie

Why You Should Read It

Lesson Objective

Students will learn how to prepare, plan, and create short, one-minute videos persuading audiences to read particular books.

Materials and Preparation

- one iPad per student
- one teacher iPad and projection or streaming technology
- "Why You Should Read It" Movie Template (one handout for each student)
- library books

Create your own "Why You Should Read It" movie.

Opening/Input

1. Launch the iMovie app.
2. Play your "Why You Should Read It" movie in front of the entire class.
3. Open up your iMovie project and show how you created all five elements.
4. Go over the "Why You Should Read It" Movie Template, step by step. Let your students know they need to complete this template before they are permitted to start creating their project using iMovie.

The Five Requirements of the "Why You Should Read It" iMovie Project:

1. Show at least 15 seconds of the book cover.
2. Mention the title and the author of the book.
3. Give a brief synopsis of the book without revealing the entire plot. (This should be approximately 30 seconds.)
4. Talk about why you like this book. (This should be approximately 15 seconds.)
5. End your video with the phrase, "And that's why you should read it!"

"Why You Should Read It" Movie Template

Instructions: Please read and fill out this handout completely before doing anything with your iPad.

A. Go to the school library.
B. Find a great book. Read it.
C. Write the <u>title</u> of the book here: _____
D. Write the <u>author</u> of the book here: _____
E. Write a <u>short synopsis</u> of the book here: _____
F. Write <u>why you like the book</u> here: _____
G. Ask your teacher to review and approve this template. Teacher's Initials: _____
H. Create your iMovie.

Remember: Your iMovie cannot be longer than one minute. No exceptions. You also must end the video with the phrase: "And that's why you should read it!"

Guided Practice

Pass out the "Why You Should Read It" Movie Template handout and have a different volunteer read each step aloud to the class.

On Their Own

1. Students must first complete their "Why You Should Read It" templates.

2. Once you have approved their templates, encourage students to rehearse what they are going to say during their book reviews. Students should be comfortable with their reports BEFORE they are given access to an iPad.

3. Since they need to shoot video, it may be helpful to pair students with other classmates. Students can take turns holding the iPad camera for one another.

4. Have students use iMovie to film, edit, and save their movies. If time permits, allow students to add music and sound effects to their movies.

Extensions

*   Assign small groups to read the same book and then work together to create a final iMovie. Each person can be responsible for a different aspect of the final product. Host a "Red Carpet" event to share the movies with the rest of the class.

*   Extend the length of the movie by several minutes. Ask students to focus on a particular literary device or comprehension strategy, and ask students to read specific examples from the text.

*   Include the participation of a lower grade classroom to act as an audience for a "Book Show" in which the young children watch each video projected on the screen. The students can then vote on their favorite. This is a wonderful way to encourage reading.

Description

Keynote is Apple's presentation app. Keynote presentations can be exported as PDFs, Keynote files, or Microsoft® PowerPoint files. In addition, Microsoft PowerPoint files can be opened as Keynote files.

How to Create a Keynote Presentation

1. Launch the Keynote app.

2. Tap the "plus" icon in the upper-left corner and select Create Presentation.

3. Choose from one of the themes displayed. Keynote gives you an array of themes from which to choose. Beginners should choose one of the first three themes in the top row.

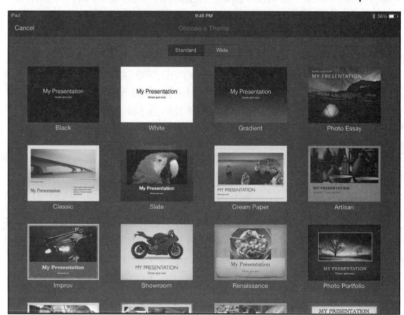

4. The first slide shown is a title slide. Double-tap inside the first text box and title your presentation.

TAGS

Free

Classroom Contexts: Whole Class, Teacher Research, Individual, Small Group

Wi-Fi: optional (for sharing files)

Grades: 3, 4, 5, 6

Prerequisites: familiarity with Mail, Camera, and Safari apps

Developer: Apple Inc.

App Version: 2.5.2

How to Create a Keynote Presentation *(cont.)*

5. To add a new slide, tap on the boxed "plus" icon in the bottom-left corner of the screen. This produces a selection tray of different slide layouts. Choose the layout that suits you.

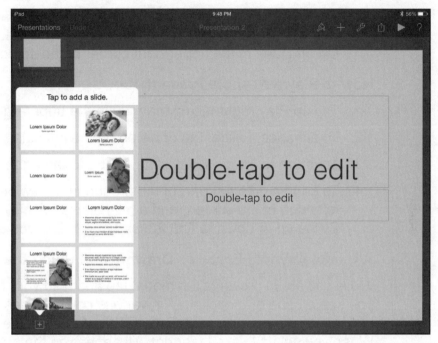

6. Tap on the "plus" icon in the upper-right corner of the screen to see a set of options, which includes adding images, shapes, or text. Use pinch and zoom to resize shapes. To resize images, tap on the image to reveal small blue guide dots. Drag these dots to resize the image.

KEYNOTE

How to Create a Keynote Presentation *(cont.)*

7. When you are finished adding text and images, tap on Presentations in the upper-left corner of the screen. This will take you back to the file view screen.

8. Tap on the default name beneath the thumbnail image of your newly created Keynote presentation. Enter the name for the file. Once you are finished, tap on Done in the upper-right corner of the screen.

How to Play a Keynote Presentation

1. Tap on Play (right-facing triangle) in the upper-right corner of the screen.

2. To advance a slide, tap or swipe on the left side.

3. To return to the previous slide, swipe to the right.

4. To go to a different part of the presentation, swipe your finger from the left edge of the screen, and a mini display of all your slides will appear. Swipe up or down to find the particular slide you are looking for.

A Useful Keynote Feature: Drawing and Using the Laser Pointer

While you are in presentation mode, tap and hold your finger on the screen until you see a pane of "pencil tips" in various colors. These allow you to draw on your slides during a presentation. On the far left is the "laser pointer" option. When you select this, a laser dot will appear on the audience's projected screen. Use this option to draw attention to a specific area on a slide.

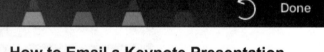

How to Email a Keynote Presentation

1. Tap on the "share" icon.

2. Select Send a Copy.

3. Choose your desired format—Keynote, PDF, or PowerPoint.

4. Select Mail.

5. A new message will appear. Enter a recipient, subject line, and message.

Travel Log

Lesson Objective
Students will learn how to research data and present it in engaging presentations.

Materials and Preparation
- one iPad per student
- one teacher iPad and projection or streaming technology
1. Prepare a Travel Log Research Template (you can use the example below).
2. Research a country (not the United States).
3. Create a Keynote presentation based on your findings.
4. Gather facts on the United States.

Travel Log Research Template

Name and map of country	Name of the capital city with a picture
Land area	Picture of the flag and currency
Total population	Some of the country's highlights

Opening/Input
1. Remind students how important it is to learn about other countries and cultures.
2. Tell students that they will be creating travel logs on any countries they choose.
3. Show students your travel log. Point out how each slide presents a different characteristic of the country.

Guided Practice
1. Share the Travel Log Research Template and the previously prepared facts on the United States. As a class, complete the template.
2. Show students how to research the rest of the Travel Log Research Template topics by doing a Safari search.
3. Ask for volunteers to help create a Keynote presentation on the United States. At the front of the room, each student should create a slide using the information from the Travel Log Research Template.

On Their Own
1. Support students as they research their countries and complete the Travel Log Research Template.
2. Have students create their own travel log slide presentations.
3. Tell students to email their travel log to you.
4. Ask for volunteers to share their presentations with the class.

App-Smashing
- Allow students to use the Barefoot World Atlas app to research their countries.
- Have students use Skitch to annotate their slides.

Third-Party Apps

This section introduces features of third-party apps. Third-party apps are apps designed by developers other than Apple and can be downloaded from the App Store. These apps may require Wi-Fi and may cost a nominal fee. These recommended apps are well suited to help you deliver practical, engaging classroom lessons.

ART LAB BY MoMA

Description

The Art Lab app provides opportunities for open-ended exploration and creativity, as well as connections to MoMA's collection. Students can use the app with a classmate, a teacher, a parent/caregiver, or on their own. There are many interactive learning activities and prompts for creativity.

Note: Your Artwork May Be Used by The Museum of Modern Art (MoMA)

This app contains a feature that enables users to share their art with The Museum of Modern Art. The museum may choose to use submitted projects for their own purposes. If you share your art, please read the disclaimer below:

By sharing your artwork with The Museum of Modern Art (MoMA) or by enabling the app so that your child can share his or her art with us, you are granting MoMA a perpetual, irrevocable, fully paid worldwide right and license to display the artwork on MoMA.org, share it with the world via social media, reproduce it and distribute it in any and all media, use it for promotional, advertising, and any other purposes, and modify or change it and authorize others to do the same, for any and all purposes. If you do not agree to these terms, please do not submit your artwork to MoMA. If you do agree, please identify yourself only by first name, age, city, and country (none of which are required for submission). We regret that we cannot notify you if we intend to use your artwork. For more information, please review our Privacy Policy at MoMA.org/privacy.

©The Museum of Modern Art, New York

ART LAB BY MoMA

How to Create an Art Project

1. Tap on the green "light bulb" icon in the upper-left side of the screen. You will get a prompt that suggests an activity to complete for your first art project. There are seventeen different ideas to choose from. As you swipe to the left to see the various ideas, you will notice the activities progress from simple to more advanced. Tap on the "speaker" icon at the top of the page to hear the text that is displayed. Press Go to begin an activity.

2. Tap on one of the shapes from the bottom of the screen to have it appear on the easel.

3. Pinch, zoom, and use two-finger tap to rotate the shapes.

ART LAB BY MoMA

How to Create an Art Project *(cont.)*

4. Tap on the "color-wheel" icon in the bottom-right corner of the screen to choose different colors.

5. You can also hold down your finger on a shape to access the edit panel. This will allow you to duplicate, delete, or make other adjustments to the shape.

6. Change the background color by tapping on the "double-square" icon on the right of the screen.

7. Start a new art project by tapping on the "plus" icon. Your art will be saved to the gallery.

8. If you need to clear the screen, select the "trash can" icon.

9. Tap on the "camera" icon on the right side of the screen at any time to save your drawing to the gallery.

How to Share and Email an Art Project

1. Go to iPad Settings. On the left side of the screen, scroll down until you find the Art Lab app and select it.

2. Tap on the slider to enable all sharing options (you only have to do this once).

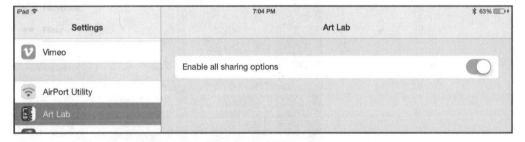

3. Return to the Art Lab app and tap on the "view gallery" icon (it looks like three squares) on the left side of the screen.

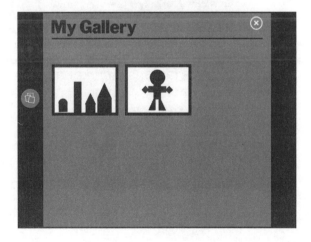

ART LAB BY MoMA

How to Share and Email an Art Project
(cont.)

4. Select any of your previously saved art projects by tapping on the image.

5. Tap on the "share" icon.

6. Select E-mail and follow the steps to email the file.

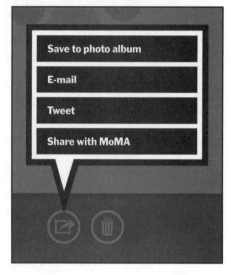

How to Browse and Play the Art Lab Activities

1. Tap on the orange "activities" icon on the left side of the screen (it looks like a pair of scissors crossed with a pencil).

2. Browse the different activities. Notice that each activity first provides as an example a famous piece of art with a detailed description of the artist and his or her work. Tap on the "speaker" icon at the top of the screen to have the text read aloud for you.

3. Select Go to begin the guided activity.

4. You may want to preview the activities to become familiar with the various steps and to ensure they are at an appropriate level for your students.

ART LAB BY MoMA

An Exquisite Corpse

Lesson Objective

Students will develop an appreciation for works of art by learning about a specific artistic technique and then collaborating on a collection of original art pieces.

Materials and Preparation

- one iPad per student
- one teacher iPad and projection or streaming technology

Make a list dividing your class into groups of three, if possible. Groups of two is an acceptable alternative.

Opening/Input

1. Launch the Art Lab app.
2. Tap on the orange "scissors and pen" icon on the left side of the screen. Next, scroll down and select "Create an 'Exquisite Corpse.'" Discuss the definitions of *exquisite* and *corpse*.
3. Read the text on the Activities page to familiarize the students with the artists and the unique techniques they used to create *Figure*.
4. Select the "Go" icon to use this artistic technique to create an original "exquisite corpse."

Guided Practice

1. Invite three volunteers to come to the front of the room and go through the directions, step by step. Allow each student to draw his or her own portion of the figure without the other two looking. One student will draw a head and neck, one student will draw a body, and the last student will draw legs and feet.
2. Discuss how there will be differences in each "exquisite corpse" but that there is no right or wrong way to create a figure. Encourage students to be creative and think outside the box.
3. With partners, have students create figures and show the final results to nearby groups. If time, have them share the results with the entire class.

On Their Own

Ask students to launch the Art Lab app and work with a partner to make their own unique collaborative art pieces. Each student should take turns holding his or her iPad so that the partner can't see what he or she is drawing. Not until the grand reveal at the end will the students know how their "exquisite corpse" looks. Allow students to create multiple figures, but ask them to save only their top two.

Extension

Art Lab provides a variety of art activities for your students to try. Just select the orange "scissors and pen" icon on the left side of the screen to view the various options.

Creatures of Light

Description

Creatures of Light is a life-science app developed by the American Museum of Natural History that helps students learn about bioluminescent creatures. It explores the diversity of organisms that glow and produce their own light. Using the latest exhibits from the American Museum of Natural History, this app introduces how scientists study this amazing natural phenomenon.

The Exhibition

Start with the first menu item called The Exhibition. This gives an overview of *Creatures of Light: Nature's Bioluminescence*, an exhibition organized by the American Museum of Natural History. Several interactive slides introduce the various topics and creatures covered in the museum exhibit. Use this part of the app to introduce bioluminescence and to discover what piques the interests of your students.

How to View the Exhibition

1. Launch the Creatures of Light app.
2. Select the Exhibition menu button on the right side of the screen.
3. Read and follow the instructions on each slide.
4. Once you have finished exploring the exhibition, press the "home" icon to return to the main screen.

How to Browse the Creatures of Light

1. Launch the Creatures of Light app.
2. Select one of the five other themes by tapping on an icon on the right side of the screen. The five themes include Enchanted Evening, Light on Land, A Sparkling Sea, Altered Light, and The Deep Ocean.
3. Choose a theme/icon, and then follow the instructions.
4. The rest of the app is self-explanatory: Pick a theme, and then swipe through the various panels as indicated with animated arrows. Watch and listen to the sounds and explanations. Use headphones or earbuds to get the best experience.
5. As there is no right or wrong order to these themes, encourage students to explore on their own and report back what they find to be most exciting and interesting.
6. You can always tap on the "home" icon in the upper-left part of the screen to get to the beginning of the app. In the upper-center part of the screen is an iOS-style progress indicator to let you know where you are in the theme. Toggle the sound by tapping on the "speaker" icon in the upper-right part of the screen. Additional interactivity is indicated with orange-colored text instructions.

CREATURES OF LIGHT

Let's Learn About the Deep Ocean

Lesson Objective

Students will click on the "Deep Ocean" icon and learn about bioluminescence as a scientific phenomenon and the bioluminescent creatures that live in this strange and wonderful habitat. Students will also learn the unique characteristics of the different light zones of the ocean. Finally, they will make a poster describing how bioluminescent light is used in the predatory cycle of a Hawaiian bobtail squid.

Materials

- one iPad per student
- one set of headphones or earbuds per student
- one teacher iPad and projection or streaming technology
- one speaker system to plug into your iPad
- poster paper and colored pens
- Deep Ocean Project Checklist (see below)

Opening/Input

1. Share the lesson objective with the class.
2. Launch the Creatures of Light app.
3. Go through the Exhibition section with the class.
4. Pass out the Deep Ocean Project Checklist.
5. Select the Deep Ocean theme and swipe through each screen, highlighting the different sections.

Deep Ocean Project Checklist

A. Define *bioluminescence*.
B. Describe the three light zones of the ocean.
C. What is the name of the <u>shallowest</u> zone?
D. What is the defining characteristic of this zone?
E. What kinds of creatures live in this zone?
F. What is the name of the <u>second</u> zone?
G. What is the defining characteristic of this zone?
H. What kinds of creatures live in this zone?
I. What is the name of the <u>deepest</u> zone?
J. What is the defining characteristic of this zone?
K. What kinds of creatures live in this zone?
L. Read about the Hawaiian bobtail squid.
M. Make a poster showing how the Hawaiian bobtail squid uses light to capture prey.

CREATURES OF LIGHT

Guided Practice

Have your students launch the app and discuss the Deep Ocean Project Checklist. Monitor students as they navigate their way through the Deep Ocean content, and have them work with partners to define *bioluminescence*, *counterillumination*, and *quorum sensing*. Discuss definitions with the class, and choose a class definition for each word.

On Their Own

Students must complete the Deep Ocean Project Checklist on their own. Provide poster paper and pens for students to create their final posters.

Extensions and App-Smashing

- The Deep Ocean Project is based on one of the five themes of this app. Students can always do a second or third project based on a different theme. Provide a list of questions for them to answer by searching the app, or give them the opportunity to write questions for each other.

- You can have your students app-smash by taking screenshots of different screens and using these still shots in iMovie to further elaborate on a given topic.

- Have students record answers to the questions from the Deep Ocean Project in Pages files. Email the documents to the teacher when finished.

- Have students use a drawing app (such as Art Lab by MoMA) to produce the final poster. Then have them email the file to a shared classroom file or email account.

BAREFOOT WORLD ATLAS

Description

This is a beautifully illustrated interactive world atlas. Since the entire atlas is downloaded, the interactivity is fluid and responsive. An audio soundtrack enhances the experience. This app allows students to learn about the world in a wonderfully immersive way.

Two Ways to Use the Atlas: Menus or "Globe Swiping"

Menus

One way to navigate the atlas is to search by using one of the menus.

1. First, tap on the "globe" icon in the upper-left corner of the screen. A Starter Atlas menu will appear that will allow you to search by a number of different criteria, including regions, countries, states, and even soccer teams! Most of the lists are organized in alphabetical order.

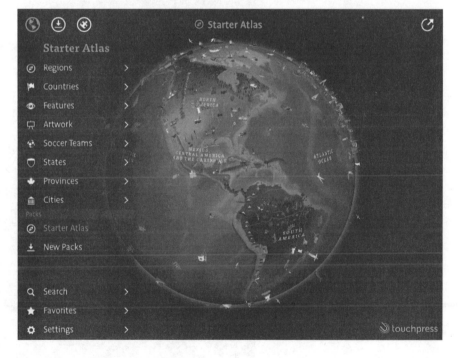

BAREFOOT WORLD ATLAS

Menus *(cont.)*

2. To locate a country, for example, select the country you want to view by tapping on Countries. An alphabetical list of countries will appear. Tap on a country, and the atlas will autoscroll to the location of the country you selected.

3. A pop-up screen on the right gives you information about the country. This information is organized into three basic parts. The upper area shows the country's shape, flag, capital city, and local time. Below, under the "i" icon tab, there is a brief description of the country. Under the "line-chart" icon tab, you are provided with numerical/statistical data, such as land area, population, currency, and highest point in the country.

BAREFOOT WORLD ATLAS

"Globe Swiping"

The second way to navigate the atlas is by swiping your finger to maneuver the globe to any point of interest.

1. Swipe a single finger to spin the globe in any direction. Tap on any country's flag to access the same data as listed on page 60.

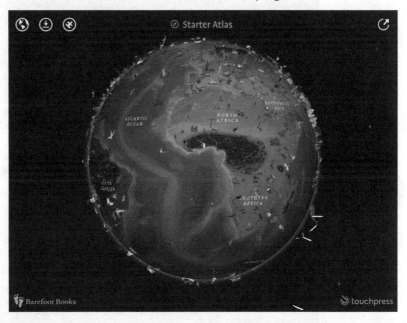

2. Besides the flags, you will notice many other animated icons as you navigate your way around the globe. These points of interest, when tapped, give a brief description in a pop-up screen to the right. Tap on the "speaker" icon at the top of the pop-up to hear the text read aloud to you.

"Globe Swiping" *(cont.)*

3. There is usually a real image associated with each point of interest. Tap on the "landscape" icon (it looks like a mountain and the sun inside of a rectangle) to access a photograph of your point of interest.

Mountain Gorilla (baby). 2011

4. To add a country or a place of interest to your Favorites folder, tap on the white star in the bottom-right corner of your screen. The star should turn yellow, which means that you can now easily access the country or place of interest in the Favorites file in the main menu.

BAREFOOT WORLD ATLAS

Something Cool in the World

Lesson Objective

Students will browse the world and search for architectural structures, animals, people, artifacts, etc. They will then gather data and create reports on individual features and share them with their classmates.

Materials

- one iPad per student
- one teacher iPad and projection or streaming technology
- one speaker system to plug into your iPad
- "Something Cool in the World" Checklist
- Skitch app

Opening/Input

1. Share the lesson objective with the students.

2. Discuss with the students the size of our planet and that people around the world share many similarities and differences. Share how the beliefs or customs of one country may seem unusual to people in a different country. Can you think of any customs you have that may seem unusual to people in another country? Discuss how differences should be celebrated and explored.

3. Launch the Barefoot World Atlas app.

4. Demonstrate how to explore the planet by "globe swiping" on the iPad. Discuss the various types of icons that appear, such as flags, people, landmarks, animals, and customs.

5. Pass out the "Something Cool in the World" Checklist.

"Something Cool in the World" Checklist

Part 1

1. Swipe around until you find something cool (something that is interesting to you). Name it here: _____

2. Collect and record all the important data about this cool location or feature.

Part 2

1. Launch Safari, and enter in the name of your cool location or feature.

2. Search and find more data about your cool location or feature. Copy or screen capture some of the data you find from your search and paste it either into a Pages document or a Google Doc™.

3. Format your document containing this new information. Make sure it has at least two to four interesting pieces of data.

BAREFOOT WORLD ATLAS

"Something Cool in the World" Checklist *(cont.)*

Part 3

1. Find the best picture you can of your cool location or feature and save it to Photos.

2. Launch the Skitch app. Use the picture you just saved to Photos, and add a title and two to three annotations describing the image. Use Skitch's arrows, text, and other tools to draw attention to the different parts of your image.

Guided Practice

Have several of your students come to the front of the room and demonstrate how to swipe around the globe using the Barefoot World Atlas app. Ask each student to tap on one cool thing that interests him or her.

On Their Own

Have your students complete Part 1, Part 2, and Part 3 of the "Something Cool in the World" Checklist. You may want to break up the three parts into different days because of the amount of work involved.

Extensions and App-Smashing

- Have your students take screenshots of different screens and use these still shots in iMovie to further elaborate on their cool things.

- Assign different groups to different continents or countries. Ask them to create travel brochures for their locations. Students should highlight interesting things about their locations, and try to convince other people to visit.

- Ask students to use the Barefoot World Atlas app to plan their next family vacation. They may visit 4–5 different locations, but they may not backtrack during their travels (they must move in one direction around the globe, ultimately ending back where they started). Ask students to record where they will travel and their reasons for visiting each location. They should collect pictures, screenshots, and interesting facts for each stop on their trips. Students can organize their plans using a Pages document or a Google Doc.

SKITCH

Description

Skitch is an efficient image-annotation tool. It can be used during a lesson to mark-up an image while teaching. It can also be used by your students to annotate images from the Web or photos they took using their devices. The annotated images can be shared, saved to the Photo Library, or opened up in another app.

How to Annotate an Image

1. Launch the Skitch app.

2. Skitch will call up your Photo Library. From here, you can select an image you want to annotate. Alternatively, you can swipe to Camera at the bottom of the screen to launch the Camera app. From here, you can snap a picture to use.

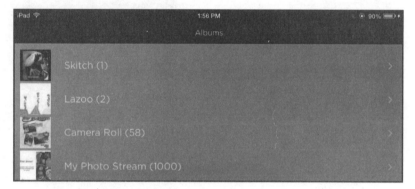

3. Tap the part of the image where you want the arrow to begin. Then, without lifting up your finger, swipe in the direction you want the arrow to point. Should you make a mistake, just tap on the "undo" icon at the top of the screen.

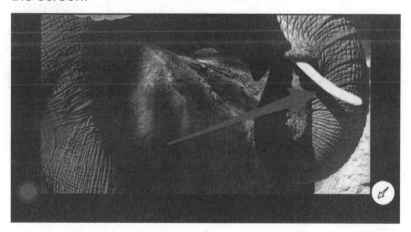

SKITCH

How to Annotate an Image *(cont.)*

4. To add text to describe what your newly created arrow is pointing at, tap the arrow button on the right side of the app. A menu will appear.

5. Select the text tool—it looks like a lowercase letter *a*.

6. Tap on the point in your image where you want your text to appear.

7. Type your text. When finished, tap outside of the text box.

8. You are now ready to share or save your newly annotated image. To do this, tap on the "share" icon. A tray of sharing options will appear. To save the image, swipe to Save at the bottom of the screen. Several save options will appear.

SKITCH

Other Useful Skitch Tools

There are many other useful tools you can select to mark-up images. The menu to the right of the screen includes a list of these features:

- a blurring tool to make your students' faces blurry (to protect their identities)

- emoticons

- a stamp tool (for "X marks the spot")

- a free-form drawing tool

- a shape tool

The menu to the left of the screen includes these features:

- eight colors

- five line thicknesses

The menu at the top of the screen includes these features:

- undo

- crop

- rotate

- clear all annotations

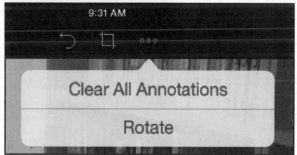

SKITCH

Science Cycles

Lesson Objective

Students will learn how to manipulate an image using annotation tools. They will then share this image using Mail.

Materials and Preparation

- one iPad per student
- one teacher iPad and projection or streaming technology

1. Take a picture of a diagram showing the life cycle of a plant. Save the image to your Photo Library.

2. Take a picture of a diagram showing the water cycle. Send this picture to each student's Mail address. Have students save the image to their Photo Libraries.

Opening/Input

1. Launch the Skitch App.

2. Select the picture of the life cycle of a plant from your Photo Library.

3. Annotate the image with an arrow by indicating the different stages of a plant's development and how it progresses from one step to the next.

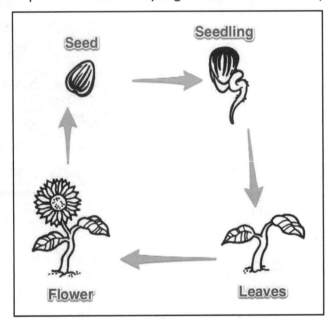

Guided Practice

Pick a volunteer to demonstrate the activity again in front of the rest of the class. Make sure you emphasize the undo button at the top center of the app in anticipation of your students making mistakes.

Science Cycles *(cont.)*

On Their Own

1. Have students annotate a picture of the water cycle.

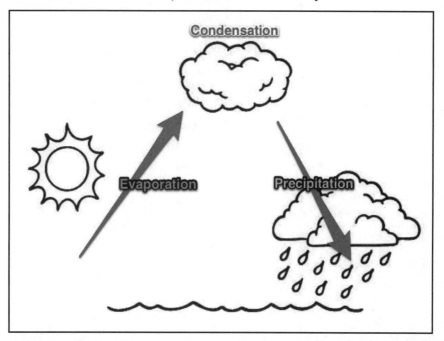

2. Once they are finished, have them email you the annotated image.

3. Share some of these emailed annotated images with the rest of the class.

Extensions

*   Have your students annotate an image of the layers of Earth.

*   Create a search game using other pictures. Take pictures of your school, and give students a list of things or places to find and label.

*   Have students take pictures of themselves in order to annotate different parts of their bodies.

PICCOLLAGE

Description

This is an easy-to-use collage app. It's great for creating scrapbook-like collages. This app is one of the fastest and easiest tools for combining images, short text, and stickers on a single page.

How to Create a Collage

1. Launch the PicCollage app.

2. Tap the center of the screen to create a new collage.

3. The rest is simple and fairly straightforward. Tap anywhere on the screen to add photos, text, videos, or stickers. You can even search for photos on the Web with PicCollage's own in-app browser.

PICCOLLAGE

How to Create a Collage *(cont.)*

4. When adding photos, you are allowed to select one or more images from Photos. After selecting the photos you want to include in your collage, tap on the "check" icon in the top-right corner of the screen. The photo(s) can then be resized, moved, or even tilted to an angle you prefer.

5. To access the camera and take a new picture for your collage, tap Photos and then tap on the "camera" icon in the top-left corner.

How to Edit Your Photos in a Collage

1. Double-tap the photo.

2. You can edit the photo, edit the border, duplicate the photo, set the photo as the background image of the whole collage, add the photo to your collection, or trace an outline of the part of the photo you want to keep.

3. If you get lost, select the large "?" button at the top center of the screen.

Layouts & Backgrounds in PicCollage

You can choose from a number of layout templates to help you organize your photo collage. Just tap on the icon in the lower-left corner of the screen and choose from one of the provided layouts. When you find a layout you like, tap on the "check" icon to apply it to your collage. To add a fun background design, tap on a space in the background. Tap on the Background icon in the window that appears, and an array of design options will appear in the bottom of the screen. Tap on a pattern to preview it, and then tap the "check" icon to save it.

Final Sharing Options

Your collages can be shared to social networks such as Facebook and Twitter, or to file-sharing services such as Google Drive, Box.net, and Dropbox. To share your collage, tap on the "share" icon (it looks like a box with an arrow pointing upward) in the bottom-right corner of the screen. Here you will be given several options, including:

- adding a caption about the collage.
- saving it to your Photo Library.
- sending it to other apps ("app-smashing").
- sending it by email.
- turning it into a greeting card that will be printed and shipped anywhere.

Mystery Collage

Lesson Objective

Students will apply design and layout skills as they create one-page collages of close-up images and creative text. Students must use their inferencing skills to correctly identify mystery objects.

Materials

- one iPad per student
- one teacher iPad and projection or streaming technology

Opening/Input

1. Share the lesson objective with the students.
2. Launch the PicCollage app.
3. Using a projector, demonstrate how to add photos, text, stickers, etc.
4. Show how you can edit photos by resizing and moving photos around.

Guided Practice

1. Ask each student to think of a specific theme and then imagine items that help identify that theme. For example, if using the theme "soccer," some items that help identify that theme would be a soccer ball, cleats, shin guards, and a net. Encourage students to share some of their own examples.
2. Next, tell students to look around the classroom and identify a new theme. It can be anything: shapes, colors, subject matter, etc.
3. Ask students to use their devices to take three or four photos of items in the classroom that are related to their selected themes. For example, if a student decides his or her theme is "circles," then he or she may decide to take a picture of the clock, a coin, and an image of the moon on the wall.
4. Using PicCollage, have students make collages using their images and at least one line of vague text (providing some sort of hint).
5. Allow students to walk around the class and share their collages with other students. Can they guess the themes? Share a few with the entire class.

On Their Own

1. Have your students identify a mystery object that they want to feature from the classroom.
2. Once they have identified their objects, have each student take three or four very close-up pictures of it with his or her iPad camera.
3. Using the PicCollage app, students need to add the three mystery photos and at least two lines of vague text to their collages.
4. Before submitting the assignment, students need to arrange all the elements of their collages in a fun and visually creative way.
5. Create a slideshow of all the different completed collages. Have a contest to see who can identify the most mystery objects.

Extension

If students have just finished a chapter of a story, they can create collages of the key elements of the story using pictures and text.

PAPER BY FIFTYTHREE

Description

Paper by FiftyThree is an innovative drawing app. It was Apple's App of the Year in 2012. The smart interface keeps the app clutter free. Included with the app is a helpful in-app tutorial, highlighting many of the app's features.

Overview

- There are three available views for the three included journals: a Journal view (main screen), a Pages view (journal is open), and a Drawing view (selected page is open). Tap and pinch to get in and out of these three views. Specifically, tap on a journal to get to a Pages view and then tap on a page to get to the Drawing view. The Drawing view is the place to start drawing.

Journal View

TAGS

Free

Classroom Contexts:
Whole Class, Individual, Small Group

Wi-Fi: optional (for sharing files)

Grades: all

Prerequisites:
familiarity with the Mail app

Developer:
FiftyThree, Inc.

App Version: 2.3.1

PAPER BY FIFTYTHREE

Pages View

Drawing View

PAPER BY FIFTYTHREE

Overview *(cont.)*

- To add a journal or page, select the "plus" icon on the appropriate screen.

- To delete a journal or page, select the "x" icon on the appropriate screen.

- To organize your journals with file names and book-cover images, tap on the "i" button on each journal.

How to Share and Save Drawings

- From the Journal or Pages view, tap on the "share" icon to view several sharing options. In Journal view, you can send the entire journal containing multiple drawings. In Pages view, you can send individual drawings.

- To save your drawing(s) to the Camera Roll, tap the "Camera Roll" icon. To email your drawing(s), tap on the "envelope" icon. To create a PDF, tap on the "App Store" icon.

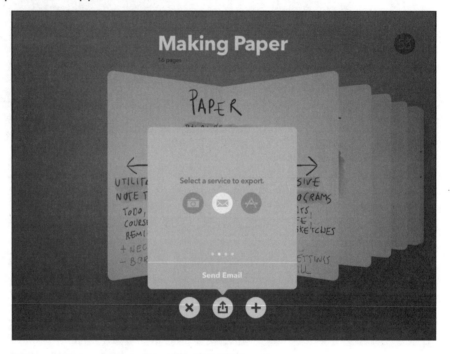

How to Draw Using Paper by FiftyThree

- Tap on the Pages view to start drawing. Use your finger to draw after you've selected a drawing tool. The faster you make your strokes, the thicker the line.

- Select different colors from the color tray in the bottom-right corner of the screen.

- Spread two fingers apart to zoom in close to your drawing without losing your place on the page. This allows you to draw fine details. Tap anywhere out of the circle to turn off the zoom feature.

- Each drawing is automatically saved in a journal.

PAPER BY FIFTYTHREE

Draw a Scene

Lesson Objective

Students will learn how to draw pictures and share them with others. Specifically, they will illustrate a scene from a preselected piece of literature.

Materials and Preparation

- one iPad per student
- one teacher iPad and projection or streaming technology
- copy of teacher-selected scene from a relevant literature selection

The teacher should select a specific scene from a piece of literature that is currently being studied in class. As the students will be drawing a scene based only on descriptions from the text, a passage with a high amount of vivid imagery should be chosen. Fewer details in the story mean more inferences by the reader and illustrator.

Opening/Input

1. Begin by discussing books the students enjoy that include illustrations. Ask the class if the illustrations added to or took away from their overall reading experiences. What impact does an illustration have on the overall story? Are there any books the students enjoyed that didn't have illustrations but they wished did?

2. Discuss how illustrations can have both a positive and negative impact on the reader, depending on the story and the illustrator. If the illustrations add to the overall reading experience, they can be an important part of the story. However, if the characters are illustrated poorly, inaccurately, or not as you imagined them in your head, this can take away from the reading experience.

3. Tell students that they are going to have the opportunity to improve a book that was recently read in class. They will be illustrating a specific scene by using the words from the page(s) to guide their drawings. Remind them the importance of matching the details in the illustration with the written details on the page.

Guided Practice

1. Read an excerpt from a book read and discussed in class. Allow the class to find details in the passage that can be included in an illustration.

2. Collect and organize all of the details from the reading passage using a graphic organizer. Remind students that a little inferencing will likely be necessary, but the illustration should be as close to the written description as possible.

3. Using the Paper by FiftyThree app, demonstrate how to open a new file and use the various drawing tools. Allow students time to become familiar with the app.

PAPER BY FIFTYTHREE

Guided Practice *(cont.)*

4. Begin illustrating the discussed excerpt, crossing off the details from the graphic organizer as you go. When you feel the class is ready, allow them time to create their own illustrations. When most have finished, allow students to share and critique (accuracy, not artistic ability) selected drawings.

On Their Own

1. Produce a new reading excerpt and ask students to become illustrators for the text. Similar to the example used in the guided practice, the excerpt should be rich in detailed descriptions and specifics.

2. Ask each student to collect as many details as possible from the reading passage and then arrange them using a graphic organizer.

3. Using the Paper by FiftyThree app, have students create new files and then illustrate the provided scene.

4. When finished, each student should save his or her illustration and email it to the teacher. The teacher can review the illustration, add comments or a grade, and then email the file back to the student.

Extensions

- Choose a scene from the same story that doesn't provide as many descriptive details. Encourage students to use their inferencing skills to "fill in the blanks" and illustrate the scene.

- Allow students to choose their own scene from the same book and then illustrate it using the same steps as listed above. Give students time to share their illustrations and see if the rest of the class can correctly identify the illustrated scenes.

- Students can use the app to create picture books. Give them specific parameters or allow them to be as creative as they want. Challenge them to tell a story using only illustrations.

App-Smashing

- Have students draw pictures of their favorite animals, save them to their Camera Rolls, and then use the Skitch app to annotate them with labels denoting the parts of their bodies.

- Using a selection of three to four images, create a "digital-video-introduction" using iMovie.

GOOGLE DOCS

Description

Google Docs is a word-processing app with some interesting features. It has basic editing features (text only, no image embedding) for creating and editing typical documents that you and your students would use in the classroom. One unique feature of Google Docs is the ability to share and edit documents with other people in real-time. Students can work together on multiple devices to create or edit a single shared document.

You need a Google email account to use Google Docs.

First things first. In order to use Google Docs, you and your students must first sign up for Google email accounts (Gmail). You can create a class Gmail account that can be shared by all of your students, but this limits collaboration and isn't recommended. Collaboration and peer editing is what Google Docs does best!

If you decide to create a Gmail account for each of your students, keep a file with their passwords handy. This set-up process can be a bit of a chore, but in order for Google Docs to be most effective, you need to take this step.

How to Create a Google Doc

1. Launch the Google Docs app.

2. Tap on the "plus" icon in the bottom-right corner of the screen.

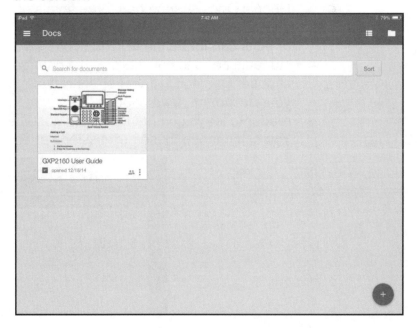

TAGS

Free

Classroom Contexts: Whole Class, Teacher Research, Individual, Small Group

Wi-Fi: required

Grades: 3, 4, 5, 6

Prerequisites: none

Developer Info: Google, Inc.

App Version: 1.2.6448

How to Create a Google Doc *(cont.)*

3. Name the file, and then tap Create.

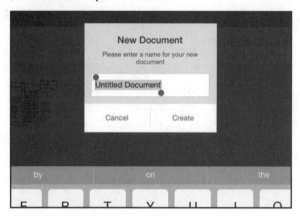

4. Now you can start typing text. You will notice that there is no saving function. As long as you don't delete the file, it will constantly autosave.

Collaboration and Peer Editing

A Google Doc created by one student can be shared with others. You can use a Google Doc for an assignment that requires collaboration with other students. You can also share a Google Doc to allow someone to peer-edit using the Commenting feature. Sharing a Google Doc gives those whom you share it with permission to modify your document in some way.

What permissions are right for you?

Google Docs sharing has three levels of permissions: can view, can edit, and can comment. "Can view" only allows others to view your document; changes or edits cannot be made. Think of it as a "read only" setting. If you or your students need to collaborate and change the contents of a document, then choose "Can edit." If you or your students need to have someone peer-edit your document, then choose "Can comment." "Can comment" allows the reader to leave comments on the document without being able to change it. You can change these permissions at any time.

GOOGLE DOCS

How to Share/Collaborate with a Classmate

1. Launch the Google Docs app.

2. Tap on the "three dots" icon in the top-right corner of the screen to share and export a document.

3. Tap on Share & export.

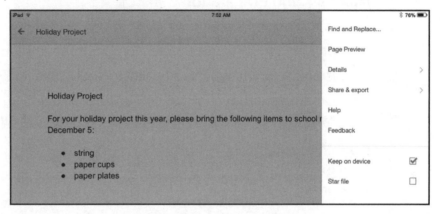

4. Tap on the "share" icon (it looks like a person with a little plus near its head) in the upper-right corner of the screen.

5. Share by entering the names or email addresses of your classmates.

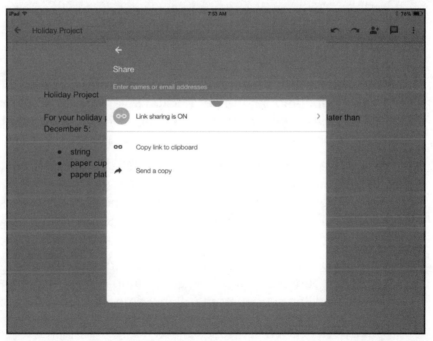

6. Choose the level of permissions for this document: can view, can edit, or can comment. Remember that "Can view" means the person can view but cannot edit your document; "Can edit" means the person can view and edit your document; "Can comment" means the person can view and comment on your document.

GOOGLE DOCS

Real-Time Collaboration Task

Lesson Objective

Students will learn how to collaborate on a single project using Google Docs to share and edit text electronically from separate devices.

Materials and Preparation

- one iPad per student
- one teacher iPad and projection or streaming technology

1. Prepare for the lesson by dividing your class into groups of three (or four).
2. Create separate information packets for each student. Make sure that no two students in a group share the same information.

Opening/Input

1. Share the lesson objective with the students, and explain the importance of collaboration.
2. Launch the Google Docs app.
3. Demonstrate how to create a new document.
4. Explain the three levels of sharing with a Google Doc.
5. Then, go over the steps necessary to share and collaborate with a classmate. Emphasize the purpose of each level of permission.

Guided Practice

1. Using a projector to enlarge your iPad screen, create a simple Google Doc and set the permission level to "can edit." Have a volunteer from the class demonstrate how to access and then edit the document displayed on the screen.
2. Have the students work in small groups of three or four to collaborate on a practice document. Assign each group a specific activity (such as checking for punctuation, capitalization, missing content, etc.). The activity can be simple, as the main goal is to practice collaborative editing. Allow students to make changes to the shared document.
3. Discuss the final edited document with the class. How did it change? Is it better or worse? Was working collaboratively an effective strategy for editing a document? Allow time for students to share their experiences.

On Their Own

1. Divide your class into predetermined groups of three or four.
2. Pass out separate information packets to each student. Each member of each group should be given different, nonoverlapping information about a famous historical figure. (If you would prefer to use content that is more relevant in your classroom, the activity can be just as effective!)

GOOGLE DOCS

On Their Own *(cont.)*

3. Have students return to their desks. One member of the group will need to create a Google Doc and share it with the other two members. All three will work on their mobile digital devices simultaneously, adding the different information from their information packets to the shared document.

4. Have students meet again to discuss the final product. Encourage them to edit and organize before submitting the final product. In the end, the collaborated document should be turned in as a finished group project.

Extensions and App-Smashing

- Since Google Docs does not support images, you can have your groups take their finished Google Docs and share them using Pages. Then, in Pages, you can have the group add a few pictures to enhance the final product.

- Using a written assignment created in Google Docs, organize a peer-editing system in which each student needs to peer-edit at least two other documents. Set the documents' permission level to "can comment" so that students can add suggestions but not change the content of the document.

- Students can create a document in Pages and then app-smash to Google Docs. Remember, however, that any images will be lost in the conversion.

Teacher Tools

As teachers, locating and organizing information for a new lesson or unit can be overwhelming at times.

This section highlights a few apps that are designed to help consolidate and organize the vast amount of information provided on the Internet. Hopefully they'll make your life as a teacher a little easier, or at least a bit more organized!

Zite	ZITE

TAGS

Free

Classroom Context:
Teacher Research

Wi-Fi: required

Grade: n/a

Prerequisites:
Pocket app

Developer Info:
Zite, Inc.

App Version: 2.6

Description

Zite is a free news aggregation tool for your iPad that gives you complete control over the types of articles that appear in your newsfeed. You can choose from hundreds of topics, and indicate the topics that interest you most. Zite searches millions of articles daily and delivers to you only the most relevant, based on your interests. The app is very easy to navigate, and allows you to either browse through the articles quickly or save them to a separate app (such as Pocket) for later reading.

How to Set Up a Zite Account and Start Browsing

1. Launch the Zite app.

2. Select Sign-Up and provide the required personal information. Be sure to write down your login and password.

3. Now you need to tell Zite what topics you would like to read more about. You can select from the topics displayed, or you can go to the upper-right corner and do a search. Once you select a few topics, Zite will start populating your Feed (your browsing window).

4. The articles are displayed in an easy-to-read grid format. Swipe through the articles and read each title to determine if an article interests you or not.

5. Tap on an article that you'd like to read. You can read it in the app or save it to a separate app (like Pocket) to read it later—even without an Internet connection.

6. To save the article, select the "share" icon in the bottom-right corner of the screen. You will be given a list of choices. You can send an email of the URL or copy the URL to paste it elsewhere. You can also select Pocket. This will send the article to your Pocket app.

POCKET

Description

Pocket is a free website bookmarking tool that allows you to organize and read articles that you have previously saved from other apps and marked to "read later." Users can save to Pocket from over 800 different apps (such as Twitter, Flipboard, and Prismatic), or even from your Mac® or PC. Use Pocket with the Zite app to browse and then save articles, videos, and Web pages to view later—even when you're offline.

How to Set Up a Pocket Account

1. Launch the Pocket app.

2. Select Sign-Up and provide the required personal information. Be sure to write down your login and password.

3. If you have marked articles in Zite, then they will appear as readable articles in Pocket.

4. Browse your articles at your leisure. Once you are finished reading an article, you can either share it, delete it, or leave it on your iPad for future reference.

Use Pocket on Your Mac and PC

You can also format your Mac or PC's Web browser to be able to mark articles to be sent to Pocket. (The steps vary depending on your particular browser's characteristics, so go to *getpocket.com* to learn more about how to format your particular computer.) You can save any article that doesn't have a Pocket button by emailing the link to *add@getpocket.com*.

SHARING SERVICES

This section provides a few suggestions on how to share online some of the projects you'll be creating with your apps. Not only will this enable you to share activities and ideas with students, parents, and other teachers, but it will also prevent using up all of the memory on your iPad. Try several of these suggested sharing services to see which one works best for you.

Your iPad has its own memory capacity, but over time, this space can get filled up. The lessons and activities in this book are designed to keep your memory footprint low, but eventually memory space will become an issue. Additionally, if you are anticipating heavy video recording, you will want to set up one or all of these free services to help minimize the impact on your device.

iCloud

As of the release of this publication, iCloud.com is an Apple service that gives you a limited amount of free storage.

Being able to access Pages, Keynote, and Numbers on any computer (Mac or PC) is a huge plus. All you need is a free iCloud account. Creating an account is as easy as setting up an email account.

Dropbox

Use the Dropbox.com service when you have files that are too large (usually video clips) to share via email. Dropbox.com creates a virtual hyperlink from your iPad to a physical hard drive on a computer. Creating a free Dropbox account allows you to place any compatible file into a designated Dropbox file folder on your computer and then access the file from your iPad.

Once you have a sharing feature from the iPad app, you can choose to have that app share the file to your Dropbox account. If all of your students have one Dropbox account set up on their devices, then they can share huge files from the designated Dropbox folder on the computer with your Dropbox app on your iPad.

How to Set Up Dropbox

1. Launch Dropbox.
2. Follow the set of prompts to set up your account.

How to Upload Photos and Video Files with Dropbox

1. You should see ellipsis (three dots) to the right of the Dropbox heading. Tap on the three dots.

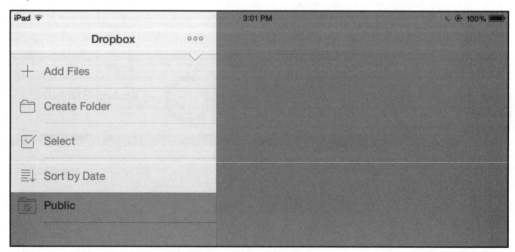

How to Upload Photos and Video Files with Dropbox *(cont.)*

2. Select Add Files. Choose the location from which you'd like to upload your photos and/or videos. They can be taken from your Camera Roll, iCloud storage, or Google Drive.

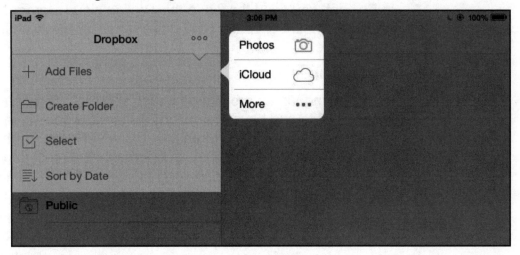

3. Tap on the photos or videos you want uploaded.

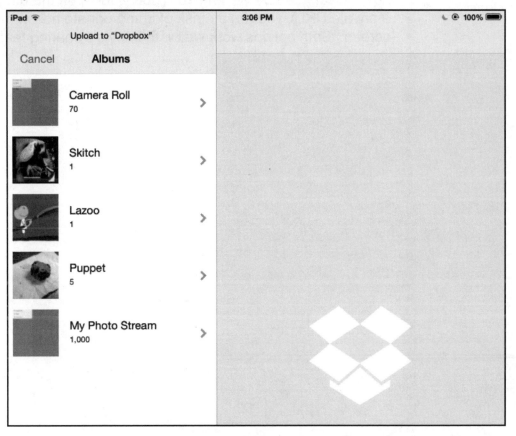

4. Once a small checkmark appears, select the Upload button (to the right of the Camera Roll heading). Your files will then upload to Dropbox.

Box.net

Box.net is similar in function to Dropbox, although you don't need a computer with designated hard-drive space to have a designated file folder. Box.net keeps your files on a virtual hard drive in the Cloud. When you share a file to Box.net, you send the file to their online cloud storage. Box.net provides a limited amount of virtual hard-drive space for free with incentives to get more space.

YouTube and Vimeo

YouTube and Vimeo are video-hosting services. Set up a free account at either website and have the option of sharing videos created by iMovie (and a selection of other apps) directly to these services. Both YouTube and Vimeo allow for customization, but probably the most important feature is the privacy settings. You can send a private URL to a parent, and only that video is available for viewing on your YouTube or Vimeo site.

The main difference between YouTube and Vimeo is that YouTube has a larger following. For your purposes as a teacher with privacy settings in play, this is not relevant. Vimeo hosts higher-quality videos and is free from advertisements. By viewing YouTube videos, on the other hand (even from a private URL), you run the risk of inappropriate ads in the margins of the screen. Both options work well with iMovie's sharing features.

iPad Accessories and Care

The iPad is an investment. It's important to know how to take care of it by using a case and cleaning the device properly. In this section, care recommendations are discussed. Suggestions regarding styli, wireless keyboards, and stands are also provided.

Styli

There are times when a stylus is useful, such as when you are drawing or taking notes. Unfortunately, styli are easily lost. For this reason, it is recommended that your students use their fingers when drawing and writing on their devices. Should you choose to use styli instead, make sure that they are iPad compatible.

External Bluetooth Keyboards

External Bluetooth keyboards are helpful when writing longer text. If you plan to do a lot of writing, get a full-sized external keyboard. The Apple wireless keyboard is durable and uses two AA batteries to stay powered.

Cases

Your school may have already made the decision to pack each iPad in a case. If so, review the documentation on the case so you can learn how to access all the ports and clean them.

If you have any input in the selection and purchasing of cases, then be sure to choose one that will protect the iPad if it is dropped.

Stands for Teacher Use

If you are using your iPad for whole-class presentations, then you need to prepare a place to house your iPad. Whether you are using a desk or podium, you want to make sure that you have easy access to your connection cables. These cables can become dislodged if the iPad is jiggled.

Cleaning the iPad

Newer iPad screens have become much more smudge resistant. Regardless, if students are working with them, the screens will still get smudged.

To clean your iPad screen, use a soft, lint-free cloth and wipe carefully. Do not use any abrasive cleaners or materials (including terry-cloth or paper towels).

For more information on how to clean and disinfect your iPad, go to *http://support.apple.com/en-us/HT3226*.

MEETING STANDARDS

Each lesson and activity meets one or more of the following Common Core State Standards © Copyright 2010. National Governors Association Center for Best Practices and Council of Chief State School Officers. All rights reserved. For more information about the Common Core State Standards, go to *http://www.corestandards.org/* or *http://www.teachercreated.com/standards/*.

CCSS.ELA-Literacy.W.3.6: With guidance and support from adults, use technology to produce and publish writing (using keyboarding skills) as well as to interact and collaborate with others.

App	How Standard Is Met	Pages
Dictionary	searching for definitions	20–21
Pages	writing, using templates	27–32
Google Docs	writing, collaborating on documents	79–83

CCSS.ELA-Literacy.W.3.8: Recall information from experiences or gather information from print and digital sources; take brief notes on sources and sort evidence into provided categories.

App	How Standard Is Met	Pages
Safari	searching for information, pasting notes	22–26
Pages	writing, using templates, pasting notes	27–32
Keynote	creating slides from Safari searches or Camera images	46–49
Creatures of Light	searching for and collecting information	56–58
Barefoot World Atlas	searching for and collecting information	59–64
PicCollage	creating collages based on Safari searches or Camera images	70–73
Google Docs	writing, pasting notes from Safari or Pages	79–83

CCSS.ELA-Literacy.W.4.6: With some guidance and support from adults, use technology, including the Internet, to produce and publish writing as well as to interact and collaborate with others; demonstrate sufficient command of keyboarding skills to type a minimum of one page in a single sitting.

App	How Standard Is Met	Pages
Mail	writing, sharing documents	11–16
Dictionary	searching for definitions	20–21
Safari	searching for articles	22–26
Pages	writing, using templates	27–32
Google Docs	writing, collaborating on documents	79–83

CCSS.ELA-Literacy.W.4.8: Recall relevant information from experiences or gather relevant information from print and digital sources; take notes and categorize information, and provide a list of sources.

App	How Standard Is Met	Pages
Safari	searching for information, pasting notes	22–26
Pages	writing, using templates, pasting notes	27–32
Keynote	creating slides from Safari searches or Camera images	46–49
Creatures of Light	searching for and collecting information	56–58
Barefoot World Atlas	searching for and collecting information	59–64
PicCollage	creating collages based on Safari searches or Camera images	70–73
Google Docs	writing, pasting notes from Safari or Pages	79–83

CCSS.ELA-Literacy.W.5.6: With some guidance and support from adults, use technology, including the Internet, to produce and publish writing as well as to interact and collaborate with others; demonstrate sufficient command of keyboarding skills to type a minimum of two pages in a single sitting.

App	How Standard Is Met	Pages
Mail	writing, sharing documents	11–16
Dictionary	searching for definitions	20–21
Safari	searching for articles	22–26
Pages	writing, using templates	27–32
Google Docs	writing, collaborating on documents	79–83

CCSS.ELA-Literacy.W.5.8: Recall relevant information from experiences or gather relevant information from print and digital sources; summarize or paraphrase information in notes and finished work, and provide a list of sources.

App	How Standard Is Met	Pages
Safari	searching for information, pasting notes	22–26
Pages	writing, using templates, pasting notes	27–32
Keynote	creating slides from Safari searches or Camera images	46–49
Creatures of Light	searching for and collecting information	56–58
Barefoot World Atlas	searching for and collecting information	59–64
PicCollage	creating collages based on Safari searches or Camera images	70–73
Google Docs	writing, pasting notes from Safari or Pages	79–83

CCSS.ELA-Literacy.W.6.6: Use technology, including the Internet, to produce and publish writing as well as to interact and collaborate with others; demonstrate sufficient command of keyboarding skills to type a minimum of three pages in a single sitting.

App	How Standard Is Met	Pages
Mail	writing, sharing documents	11–16
Dictionary	searching for definitions	20–21
Safari	searching for articles	22–26
Pages	writing, using templates	27–32
Google Docs	writing, collaborating on documents	79–83

CCSS.ELA-Literacy.SL.3.5: Create engaging audio recordings of stories or poems that demonstrate fluid reading at an understandable pace; add visual displays when appropriate to emphasize or enhance certain facts or details.

App	How Standard Is Met	Pages
iMovie	recording movies, using annotation features, adding voice-overs	33–45
Keynote	creating slides from Safari searches or Camera images	46–49
PicCollage	creating collages for iMovie and Keynote	70–73

CCSS.ELA-Literacy.SL.4.5: Add audio recordings and visual displays to presentations when appropriate to enhance the development of main ideas or themes.

App	How Standard Is Met	Pages
iMovie	recording movies, using annotation features, adding voice-overs	33–45
Keynote	creating slides from Safari searches or Camera images	46–49
PicCollage	creating collages for iMovie and Keynote	70–73

CCSS.ELA-Literacy.SL.5.5: Include multimedia components (e.g., graphics, sound) and visual displays in presentations when appropriate to enhance the development of main ideas or themes.

App	How Standard Is Met	Pages
iMovie	recording movies, using annotation features, adding voice-overs	33–45
Keynote	creating slides from Safari searches or Camera images	46–49
PicCollage	creating collages for iMovie and Keynote	70–73

CCSS.ELA-Literacy.SL.6.5: Include multimedia components (e.g., graphics, images, music, sound) and visual displays in presentations to clarify information.

App	How Standard Is Met	Pages
iMovie	recording movies, using annotation features, adding voice-overs	33–45
Keynote	creating slides from Safari searches or Camera images	46–49
PicCollage	creating collages for iMovie and Keynote	70–73

Apps:

Art Lab by MoMA, description 51

Art Lab by MoMA, lesson 55

Barefoot World Atlas, description 59

Barefoot World Atlas, lesson 63

Camera, description 18

Creatures of Light, description 56

Creatures of Light, lesson 57

Dictionary, description 20

Dictionary, lesson 21

Google Docs, description 79

Google Docs, lesson 82

iMovie, description 33

iMovie, lesson 44

Keynote, description 46

Keynote, lesson 49

Mail, description 11

Mail, lesson 14

Pages, description 27

Pages, lessons 30, 32

Paper by FiftyThree, description 74

Paper by FiftyThree, lesson 77

PicCollage, description 70

PicCollage, lesson 73

Pocket, description 86

Safari, description 22

Safari, lesson 25

Skitch, description 65

Skitch, lesson 68

Timer, description 17

Zite, description 85

iPad Basics:

care and cleaning 92

organizing apps 7

projecting images 9

restarting your device 9

screen capture 8

searching for apps 7

select, copy, and paste 8

switching between apps 7

troubleshooting 9

use and availability 5

iPad Accessories and Care:

cases and stands 92

external Bluetooth keyboards 92

styli 92

Permissions, student photos 6

Permissions, website 5

Tags:

Classroom format

individual 11, 17, 18, 20, 22, 27, 33, 46, 51, 56, 59, 65, 70, 74, 79

small group 11, 17, 18, 20, 22, 27, 33, 46, 51, 56, 59, 65, 70, 74, 79

teacher research 11, 17, 18, 20, 22, 27, 33, 46, 51, 56, 59, 65, 70, 79, 85, 86

whole class 11, 17, 18, 20, 22, 27, 33, 46, 51, 56, 59, 65, 70, 74, 79

Cost, free apps

Art Lab by MoMA 51

Camera 18

Creatures of Light 56

Dictionary 20

iMovie 33

Google Docs 79

Keynote 46

Mail 11

Pages 27

Paper by FiftyThree 74

PicCollage 70

Pocket 86

Safari 22

Skitch 65

Timer 17

Zite 85